ID0603346

In a Pickle or a Jam

In a Pickle or a Jam

Vicki Willder

CHL CREATIVE HOME LIBRARY

In Association with Better Homes and Gardens

Meredith Corporation

ABOUT THE AUTHOR

For the past sixteen years, Vicki Willder has been Director of Food Services at the Kamehameha Schools in Honolulu, Hawaii. In a life devoted to food, Miss Willder has also assisted hotel chefs in Scotland and managed a tea room in England. She studied at the Royal Polytechnic and Westminster School of Cookery in London.

Creative Home Library
©1971 by Meredith Corporation, Des Moines, Iowa
SBN 696-27500-7 Library of Congress Number 72-145623

Printed in the United States of America
photography by Bart J. De Vito

In a Pickle or a Jam

Contents

Introduction

"Something creative" is the plea of every homemaker in these days of packaged foods, frozen dinners, heat-and-serve meals. A supply of homemade jams, jellies, pickles, relishes, and chutneys will perk up everyday eating, and lend style to company dinners, too. An array of colorful shining jars on the cupboard shelf is a sheer pleasure to look at. Sandwiches become more interesting; canapés are easily assembled. Different and delicious glazes from your jellies can be put on pork, ham, and chicken. Suddenly you have a variety of sauces for casseroles, steaks, and fish, fruit syrups for puddings and ice cream, fillings for pies, cakes, and tarts.

The perfect Christmas, hostess, and house-warming gift is a fruit or vegetable preserved in your own home. These pickles and jams are also the most appreciated donation to any fund-raising project; watch and see if your homemade contribution isn't snapped up first! And whenever you are asked to bring along some food to a church supper or other large dining affair, how proud you will be to offer one of the delicious (and easy!) recipes from this book!

One more introductory thought. Do you remember the days when afternoon tea was a social custom? The polished silver, the best china, the hand-embroidered napkins, the bowls of flowers from the garden. The delicious fruitcake, the shortbread fingers, the assortment of jams and jellies in small molds, shimmering like jewels in cut-glass dishes to accompany the hot buttered toast, the aromatic tea. Somehow this delightful custom has been lost in the scramble of this modern age. Why not start your own one-woman campaign to revive this charming custom, if only in a small way. Next time you serve refreshments to the family or friends include a gemlike glass of your own homemade jelly shimmering in a pretty dish, a plate of savory sandwiches filled with one of your best chutneys, a frosty pitcher of fruity beverage made with one of your own home-bottled syrups.

You will have much fun and enjoyment in this branch of cookery where the rules are simple and the costs low.

Cooking for Fun and Profit

You certainly do not have to limit yourself to cooking a jar or two of cherry jam for selling at a bazaar. One of the nice things about fruit and vegetable preserving is the potential for conducting it on a large scale. If you and your friends or organization ever need to make a good sum of money, consider preserving as a business! It's perfect for those who like to cook and who don't want to invest money in equipment at the beginning.

Let's imagine your group has decided to give annual support to an underprivileged child in college. Before you find yourselves in a pickle or a jam, study these few hints for making your business venture a success.

1. Sit down with everyone involved and decide how much time each person can give to cooking—daily, weekly, or monthly—how much equipment you need, what premises you can use. Then check with local government officials to make sure that the premises meet government health regulations so that you can obtain a permit to operate.

2. Enlist the aid of husbands who have executive know-how just crying out to be used. Often they will want to roll up their sleeves and join in the cooking; by all means encourage them, for their cooking skills can be excellent. Other jobs for husbands are bookkeeping, advertising, designing and printing labels, carrying finished products into the stores.

3. Find out the fruits and vegetables that are grown locally. Often farmers will be happy to let your group pick your own fruit. This is an ideal situation, keeping your costs down and at the same time providing you with fruit at its best.

4. Check with local supply houses for wholesale prices on sugar, vinegar, spices, and so forth, also for jars and other equipment.

5. Check local and state sales tax laws.

6. Interview state extension-service personnel or home-economics instructors at your local high school or college, regarding recipes, popularity of fruits and vegetables, the most up-to-date cooking methods.

7. Make up a batch of tasting samples for local restaurants, delicatessens, grocery markets, and gift shops. Package the samples and price them so that you have a reasonable margin of profit. Also, give your line of pickles and jams an attractive name, preferably a local one. Why not conduct a contest among group members for your brand name?

8. Be sure to tell your story to the press in your area—a local newspaper, a church bulletin or magazine.

9. When cooking jams for profit, you should resist the temptation to double or triple a recipe. If ingredients are multiplied, the mixture will boil over and you'll have a mess on your hands. *Jams and jellies should be made in small batches.*

Packaging Your Wares

A gift from the kitchen is always appreciated at Christmas time, birthdays, showers for the bride-to-be, as a welcome for a new neighbor, as a thank-you to a hostess, as a gift just for the joy of giving. No problem here for the homemaker with a supply of jams, jellies, chutney, and marmalades lining her shelves. You can enhance the uniqueness of your present by giving some thought to the packaging.

Here are a few suggestions. When you are shopping, especially during sales or when you have spare pennies, be on the lookout for bargains in pottery, china, and glassware which make attractive containers. Glass custard cups filled with homemade jams, jellies, marmalades, or chutneys, sealed with colored paraffin, wrapped in clear cellophane, and tied with ribbon make pretty gifts. The small freezer-to-oven casserole dishes are another idea, decorated the same way. Small fluted soufflé dishes, baked-bean pots, or the ceramic coffee mugs which are now so popular all lend themselves to this use. For more elegant containers, use sets of tumblers or sherbet glasses, brandy snifters, ginger jars, fruit bowls, and milk-glass dishes which come in many shapes and can be used for many purposes in the home afterward.

You can also bargain-hunt at country auctions and in city thrift shops for small decanters to fill with fruit syrups or salad dressings. To make sure that the stoppers are tightly closed, seal tightly with transparent sealing tape, and add a card marked "refrigerate."

Plastic containers with tight-fitting lids are excellent for some relishes, chutneys, and fruit butters. However, plastic cannot be sterilized, so you must mark everything "refrigerate." And don't fill plastic containers with hot-off-the-stove recipes; let the mixture cool before filling the container, then cover it tightly with plastic wrap before refrigerating. The new disposable, plastic party-pack glasses come in many shapes, both plain and decorated. They are sturdy enough to hold any recipe that can be packed cold. Seal with clinging plastic wrap, and use a colored magic marker to write the name of the recipe and "refrigerate" right on the glass.

Have you checked your cupboards lately? Peanut butter, mayonnaise, instant coffee and tea, and honey jars make fine containers for practically everything. The shorter, chunkier soft-drink bottles are excellent for syrups; seal these bottles with corks that fit tightly. Baby-food jars are wonderful containers to save. When you have six or eight, you can fill them with different jams and jellies, wrap up prettily in a shoe box, and give a special gift pack to a special friend. These assortments of jams and jellies in baby-food jars are a good way to package if you are cooking for fund-raising projects. Be sure to sterilize any bottles or jars you use in this novel way.

As you make your jams and pickles, think ahead and pack in specially decorated containers those items you are going to reserve for Christmas gifts. Containers can be made very appealing by using attractive labels, colorful decals, red and green tape, felt appliqués pasted on with a dab of glue or touched here and there with sequins or glitter, miniature plastic and wax fruits (sold in small bunches at the dime store) glued to the top of the jar, a tiny spray of holly, lids enameled in gay colors, and so on.

If your product has been sealed with paraffin, melt a small amount of extra wax and stir in harmless food coloring to make it red and green. Pour this over the original wax covering. Before the colored wax becomes firm, decorate it with foil stars, decals, holiday seals, or cutouts from old Christmas cards. Tie on your prettiest bow, and you have a beautiful gift, a joy to give and receive.

But don't overdo the decorating. Let the brilliant natural colors of your preserves act as a foil and use the decoration only to enhance your product.

Tips on Exhibiting at Fairs

Let's assume you have made quite a few recipes in this book by now. You feel confident of your ability to cook various pickles and jams. Why not—for the fun of it—take some of your wares and enter them at the state or county fair?

For several years, I acted as a judge at country fairs in the fruit-preserving section. The display always took away my breath: the ambers and topazes of marmalades, the scarlets of strawberry and raspberry jams, the emerald of mint jelly, the earth brown of chutneys, the look of jade about watermelon pickles. Seeing jams and pickles at a fair is like standing in front of a stained-glass window, with the sunlight shining through.

I hope you decide to enter your favorite recipes in competition. If you do, here are a few tips you will find useful:

Jams made with strawberries, cherries, raspberries, and currants should contain whole fruit as evenly sized as possible, distributed throughout the preserve. Clear color is important. The aroma should be redolent of the fresh, natural, uncooked fruit, and the flavor not cloying. A good consistency in jam is determined by how easily it spreads.

Jellies should be sparkling and clear. Their flavors should be less sweet than jam. Jelly must hold its shape when spooned from a jar.

A clear bright color is most desirable with *marmalade*. The peel should be the same thickness and length, evenly distributed throughout. Judges will favor a zesty flavor. In texture, marmalade should be neither runny nor stiff.

Vegetables used in making *pickles* should be evenly diced or, if spear shaped like green beans, even in length and thickness. Pack your container firmly and cover the vegetables completely with a pickling solution that is clear and well seasoned. Judges will look for pickles that are crisp and crunchy, and flavored with authority!

The fruits and vegetables in a *relish* should be neatly chopped or diced and distributed evenly. A clear and subtle flavor is desired. In consistency relishes should be firm but not too stiff.

If a *chutney* contains curry powder, it should be a rich brown color. Try to distribute fruit and vegetables evenly. A rich, spicy, and well-blended flavor will make a good impression. The consistency should be fairly thick.

It is recommended that you make only small batches of a recipe for competition. Place in plain sterilized glasses or jars and seal neatly and firmly. Print clearly in ink the name of the product on a plain label and paste it to the side of the jar. Also paste labels on the bottoms of your jars with your name on them. Two identical jars will be required for the judges to sample for flavor, color, and consistency. It is a good idea to take along a small washcloth, a clean polishing cloth, and some extra labels. That way, you can remove finger marks, put a last-minute polish on your jars, and replace labels that fall off or get messy.

If you don't win a blue ribbon, you might get an honorable mention, which is an honor in itself. And if you win nothing, don't be downhearted. You will have gained valuable experience, made new friends, exchanged recipes, and enjoyed the general spirit of the fair. Who knows—next year you might be a prize winner.

You are all set to roll up your sleeves and get to work making a lush jam or a sparkling jelly. Keep in mind that a good jam should turn out fairly smooth since the fruit is crushed or chopped before cooking. Where pieces of fruit can be seen, they should be well distributed and a good color. Jam, sometimes labeled "preserve" when the fruit in the jam retains its shape, should be made in small batches and cooked rapidly after the sugar has dissolved.

Jelly is made by cooking fruit juice with sugar. A good jelly should be tender and spreadable, as well as firm enough to hold a shape and to quiver at the touch of a spoon. Jelly should be clear and have a sparkle quality.

Jams and Jellies

Fruits

The selection and preparation of fruits used in making jams and jellies can make a great difference in the finished product. Fruits used should be firm, ripe, and unblemished. Try to use fruit that is a little underripe, for absolutely ripe fruit is apt to be lacking in pectin. All fruits should be washed before using. Place fruits in a colander under running cold water and wash one at a time. *Never* use hot water to wash fruit. Larger fruits can be wiped with a wet cloth and dried on paper toweling.

Fruit should be processed immediately after being prepared. It deteriorates rapidly even if kept in a refrigerator tightly covered. You will not get good results if fruit is allowed to stand after preparation for any length of time.

When peeling fruit, use a stainless-steel knife or parer. Peel as thin as possible. To peel thin-skinned fruit like peaches, dip the fruit briefly in boiling water. Lift out and place in cold water, and you will find that the skin comes off easily.

To remove pits from firm fruit, cut with a stainless-steel knife. With cherries, insert a new hairpin into the fruit, moving the bent end around until you feel it lock about the stone; then pull, and the stone should slip out. Do this over the preserving pan to avoid wasting the juice.

If you do not wish to remove the pits from the raw fruit, particularly cherries, oranges, lemons, limes, and grapefruits, you can begin cooking your recipe. The pits will eventually emerge from the fruit and float to the surface where they can be easily removed with a slotted spoon.

Reserve pits and seeds removed from fruit, including orange and lemon seeds. Tie them in a piece of clean muslin or cheesecloth and boil with the fruit and sugar. *At all times* the pits should be kept in a tied bag during cooking. They are needed because they contain pectin.

Sugar

Use granulated cane or beet sugar in your cooking. Brown sugar gives a very good flavor but does not set well. Raw sugar, if available, is good with jams, but it should be avoided with jellies because it sometimes affects the setting quality or makes the jelly less clear. You may want to use 25 percent brown sugar and 75 percent granulated sugar for jam. Honey may also be used in the proportion of 25 percent honey and 75 percent granulated sugar or, for a very soft jam, 50 percent honey and 50 percent sugar.

Some cooks warm their sugar. This little process cuts down on cooking time, and the sugar dissolves more quickly so that there is less chance of crystals in the finished product. To warm sugar, spread it in a shallow pan or heatproof dish, place in a warm oven at 150 degrees, and leave for 10–15 minutes, or until warmed through.

When cooking the fruit and sugar, it is important to stir the sugar until it is dissolved completely. This will not only prevent the sugar from burning, but will prevent the finished jam from containing suspended crystals which affect texture and color.

Utensils

The proper equipment is all-important in any type of cooking. Some of the utensils already in your kitchen can do double duty.

    1. Preserving pan or kettle—stainless steel, aluminum, or enamelware kettle, about six-quart capacity. This should be large enough so that the jam or jelly can boil rapidly yet not boil over. Heavy-duty aluminum pans suitable for jam making may be found at army-surplus stores.

    2. Long-handled wooden spoon for stirring.

    3. A slotted spoon for skimming, plus one ladling spoon.

    4. A measuring cup for liquids, and one for solids.

    5. Lemon squeezer; apple corer; grater for rind of lemons, oranges, etc.

    6. Stainless-steel knife for paring, plus chef's knife for chopping.

    7. Chopping board.

    8. Colander.

    9. Hand or automatic grinder or blender.

  10. One jelly bag, which you can buy or make.

  11. China, glass, or earthenware bowls.

  12. Cheesecloth or muslin for tying spices, peel, seeds, etc.

  13. Glasses, jars, paraffin, and labels.

    If possible, reserve your preserving pans for making jams and jellies. Before using preserving pan, wash to remove any musty storage odor. Wash your wooden spoon and chopping board thoroughly after use. Dry wooden items in the open air.

Jelly Bag

Jelly bags are readily available in stores. If you would like to make your own, here are some simple directions:

Cut a piece 18 inches by 24 inches—either double or single thickness—from fine muslin or cheesecloth. Form into a cone and stitch all seams firmly. Attach four pieces of tape long enough to tie when needed to catch the drippings.

A stand usually comes with a store-bought jelly bag. If your jelly bag is homemade, suspend a broom or mop handle over the backs of two chairs, tie the bag securely to the handle and let it drip into a bowl placed beneath the bag.

Before using the bag, scald it in boiling water and wring it out as dry as possible. After use, wash thoroughly, rinse, and hang to dry in the open air.

It is a temptation to hasten the dripping of the juice by squeezing the bag when it is full of pulp. If you do this, your jelly will be cloudy. It is best to let the jelly drip overnight.

Jam Glasses and Jars

The standard jelly glass is a nice container for both jams and jellies because you can use up the contents quickly. Small-size standard preserving jars can also be used for jams and jellies. Most households accumulate glasses and jars of various shapes and sizes which can be used for your preserves when they can be properly sterilized and sealed.

To sterilize your containers, wash them clean, then cover with boiling water and simmer for 5 minutes. New rubber washers, if used, should be washed, sterilized with boiling water, and dried before using. To dry containers, place them on a baking sheet and put into the oven at 250–275 degrees. The containers should be kept in the oven until the jam is ready.

When ready for filling, stand glasses or jars on a warm plate or tray. Stir jams well and allow to cool a little before putting them in the hot sterilized containers.

Some jellies should be stirred before packing, others should not be stirred. Follow directions given in individual recipes.

Cooking and Testing for Set

Preserving is time consuming. If you want good results, organize your time so that you can complete the job without distraction. If the telephone rings or another distraction occurs, take the pan from the heat, or it may burn. Overcooked jam may not set, has bad texture, poor color, and little flavor. Undercooked jam also has poor color and flavor, is thin and runny, and ferments quickly.

Always bring your mixture to a rolling boil. This means that the contents of the preserving pan or kettle will bubble and foam, often rising considerably in the pan. (That is why it is vital that you have plenty of room in your pan, otherwise a boil-over will occur which can be messy to clean up. Do not attempt to double or triple recipes for this reason.)

Boil hard for 2 minutes, then start testing for set.

Skimming is important if you are to obtain a clear jam or sparkling jelly. A slotted spoon is best for this. Some jams or jellies produce lots of scum, so skim frequently during cooking and don't wait until the setting point is reached before starting to skim.

Testing for Set with Thermometer:

If you make a lot of jams, it is worth investing in a candy thermometer. Setting point is reached when the temperature reads 220–222 degrees; however, these temperatures vary with altitude.

For sea level, boil to 222° F
2,000 feet boil to 217° F
5,000 feet boil to 212° F
7,500 feet boil to 207° F
10,000 feet boil to 203° F
15,000 feet boil to 193° F
30,000 feet boil to 165° F

The candy thermometer should not be allowed to rest on the bottom of the pan. It should be kept suspended in the jam or jelly. After using, do not put the thermometer on a cold surface, for it is liable to break.

The Sheet Test:

The less modern but more often used method of determining whether your jam or jelly has set or jellied is to dip a cool metal spoon into the boiling mixture; lift it 12 inches above the mixture. Allow the mixture on the spoon to cool slightly, then tip the spoon sideways. When you first do this, the jelly drops will probably be thin and syrupy. As boiling continues, the jelly drops become thicker and start to run together off the spoon. Jelly reaches the setting point when the liquid stops flowing in a stream and divides into two distinct drops that run together and sheet from the edge of the spoon.

Do not wait too long to test the jam or jelly. Sometimes the set is reached very quickly. If you are using a wide pan, the liquid will evaporate rapidly, and the setting point will be reached quite soon. Also the pectin content of the fruit will affect the cooking time. High pectin content will shorten cooking time; low pectin content will lengthen it.

Remove your kettle from the heat when setting point is reached. Allow the mixture to cool and thicken slightly, then stir gently to distribute the fruit.

If you overcook a jam, one remedy is to add the juice of two lemons and bring to a boil. If this does not produce a set, bottle the syrupy mixture and use it as a sauce for puddings, a topping for ice cream, or a mix for drinks.

Filling, Sealing and Storing Glasses and Jars

Paraffin is used to seal jellies and jams. Break quarter-pound bars of paraffin into small pieces and place in top of a double boiler over hot water or in a clean, dry coffee can. If you use the coffee can, place it in a pan of hot water over low heat until the paraffin melts. *Paraffin should never be melted over direct heat.* Keep paraffin warm while waiting to use.

Pour hot jams and jellies into hot glasses to within ½ inch of the top, holding ladle close to the glass to prevent bubbles from forming. Wipe the glass clean above the jelly with a damp cloth and dry thoroughly. Cover immediately with a ⅛–¼ inch layer of *hot* paraffin. Be sure the paraffin touches all sides of the glass, but don't use more than necessary. Prick any air bubbles that appear on the paraffin. Allow the glasses to stand until the paraffin hardens, preferably overnight. Cover glasses with metal lids.

If using various shapes and sizes of jars and glasses, treat jams and jellies as indicated, adding a thin layer of paraffin before screwing on tops.

If using new standard preserving jars with good screw-on tops, pour hot jams and jellies to one-fourth inch from the top of the jars, omitting the paraffin. Wipe the top of the containers with a clean, damp cloth. Put on lids and screw the metal bands on tightly.

All filled and sealed containers must be thoroughly wiped on the outside to remove spills before they are stored; otherwise, they will attract insects. Let jams and jellies cool overnight on a rack or cloth. Then store in a place that is clean, dry, cool, and dark. Darkness is important because light affects the color of jams and jellies.

Do not store any preserves in a cupboard above a stove or radiator. The rising heat will cause them to spoil.

Label your jars with the name of the contents and the date. Use in rotation, checking jars frequently for any sign of mold. Should you spy some mold, open the jar and remove it all with a spoon. Turn the jam into a small saucepan and heat to a boil. Then use right away.

The Amount of Jam or Jelly Obtained

No exact measure can be expected from a recipe because fruit varies in pectin content. The higher the pectin content, the shorter the cooking time; hence, less evaporation and a greater yield. Also, fruit varies in the amount of juice it yields.

The size of the pan is also a factor. A shallow pan allows rapid evaporation of the liquid, so that the setting point is reached more quickly. Some jams, particularly those made with bottled or powdered pectin, require a lot of skimming which may cut down on yield.

A Word about Pectin

Why do some jams and jellies need less cooking time than others to reach the setting point? The answer is pectin, a substance which causes the jelling of fruit juices. *Without pectin, no fruit jam or jelly is possible.*

Rich in Pectin:	*Poor in Pectin:*
Apples	Strawberries
Red currants	Blueberries
Cranberries	Peaches
Gooseberries	Apricots
Plums	Cherries
Guavas	Figs
Quinces	Grapes
Lemons	Pineapple
Oranges	Rhubarb
Concord grapes	

Overripe fruit does not have so much pectin as slightly underripe fruit. The growing season will also affect the pectin and acid content of fruits. A wet growing season will lessen the pectin content; a dry season will increase it. Since estimated yield is affected by the amount of pectin present in the fruit, I find it a good idea to have a couple of spare jars ready and sterilized, in case the pectin content is unusually high.

Fruit from the garden, picked when just underripe and made immediately into jam, has a far higher setting quality than fruit bought in a market. However, extra pectin can be added in the form of apple juice, red currant juice, or lemon juice—three rich sources of pectin often added to fruits lacking this vital substance.

Tart apples for pectin:

Boil till mushy, stirring frequently, 4 green, unpeeled, coarsely chopped apples (1 pound) with 1 cup water. Allow to drip through a jelly bag overnight (do not squeeze bag). Keep refrigerated and well-sealed till needed. Windfalls are excellent apples for this.

Red currant juice for pectin:

Wash currants and stew gently in water to cover until soft. Mash and place in a jelly bag and allow to drip overnight (do not squeeze bag). As needed, add to the fruit in the proportion necessary according to the recipe you are using.

Extracting lemon juice:

Put lemons in hot water for a few minutes (this results in more juice being extracted) before cutting and squeezing. Add to recipe in proportion. Usually the juice of one or two lemons provides enough pectin and acid to set the jam.

One-half teaspoon tartaric acid or one-half teaspoon citric acid can be substituted for the juice of one lemon in any recipe needing more pectin in order to jell. Dilute the acid in a little warm juice, add to the fruit and sugar in a preserving pan, proceed to bring to a rolling boil, then test for set in the usual way.

Do not use commercial pectin (either liquid or powdered) in a recipe unless the recipe calls for it. The amount of sugar, cooking time, and general methods are quite different for different fruits and combinations of fruit. The manufacturers of commercial pectin provide recipes along with their products, and if their directions are followed faithfully, the results will be excellent. Jelly making, using liquid or powdered pectin, is quick and easy. The cooking time is much shorter, and therefore the final yield of jelly is greater.

Apple Jam

Cooking time: 2 hours

Yield: 12 8-ounce glasses

12 medium-size cooking apples,
    about 4 pounds
8 cups sugar
2 lemons, rind and juice
3 tablespoons ground ginger
4 whole cloves, tied in cheesecloth
½ cup brandy

METHOD:

1. Peel, core, and slice apples, as for a pie.
2. Combine apples, sugar, lemon rind and juice, and spices in a heavy kettle.
3. Heat to boiling. Simmer until set, about 2 hours, stirring frequently. Do not add water.
4. Remove spice bag. Stir in brandy. Seal in hot sterilized glasses.

NOTE:

Nice for apple turnovers, or as a spread for gingerbread.

Apple Jelly

Cooking time: 1 hour

Yield: 10 8-ounce glasses

12 medium-size cooking apples,
    about 4 pounds
1 cup water
8 cups sugar

METHOD:

1. Chop apples. Place apples and water in a heavy kettle.
2. Heat to boiling. Simmer until apples are soft, about 25 minutes. Place in a jelly bag and drain overnight.
3. The next day, add sugar to apple juice in the same kettle. Heat to boiling. Boil until jelly tests for set. Seal in hot sterilized glasses.

NOTE:

Apples of the cooking variety usually turn to a mush in about 25 minutes of cooking. Hasten the process by mashing during cooking with a wooden spoon.

Serve Apple Jelly with turkey or chicken.

Apple-Cherry Jam

Cooking time: 40 minutes

Yield: 10 8-ounce glasses

3 medium-size cooking apples,
    about 1 pound
½ cup water
10 cups ripe sour red cherries,
    about 2½ pounds
6 cups sugar

METHOD:

1. Peel, core, and slice apples as for pie. Tie peel and seeds in a piece of cheesecloth.
2. Combine apples and water in a heavy kettle.
3. Heat to boiling. Simmer, stirring often, until almost soft. Add cheesecloth bag and cherries.
4. Simmer until cherry pits rise to top. Remove pits with a slotted spoon. Add sugar and stir until sugar dissolves.
5. Boil rapidly until jam sets, about 10 minutes. Remove apple bag. Seal in hot sterilized glasses.

NOTE:

Try this with your breakfast toast or with hot biscuits.

Apple-Ginger Jam

Cooking time: 30 minutes

Yield: 6 8-ounce glasses

10 small cooking apples, about 2½ pounds
1 cup water
2 teaspoons ground ginger
4 cups sugar

METHOD:
1. Peel, core, and slice apples, as for pie. Tie peel and seeds in a piece of cheesecloth.
2. Combine apples and water in a heavy kettle.
3. Heat to boiling. Simmer, stirring often, until almost tender. Add cheesecloth bag and ginger.
4. Simmer until apples form a smooth pulp. Remove apple bag. Add sugar and stir until sugar dissolves.
5. Boil rapidly until jam sets, about 15 minutes. Seal in hot sterilized glasses.

NOTE:
Serve with roast pork, pancakes, and waffles.

Apple-Lemon Jam

Cooking time: 20 minutes

Yield: 5 8-ounce glasses

6 medium-size cooking apples,
about 2 pounds
1 cup water
2 lemons, rind and juice
4½ cups sugar

METHOD:
1. Peel, core, and slice apples, as for pie.
2. Combine apples, water, and lemon rind and juice in a heavy kettle.
3. Heat to boiling. Simmer, stirring often, until soft.
4. Add sugar, and stir until sugar dissolves.
5. Boil rapidly until jam sets, about 20 minutes. Seal in hot sterilized glasses.

NOTE:
Mix a little of this with tomato sauce and serve with cold beef or ham.

Apple-Lemon Jelly

Cooking time: 1 hour

Yield: 5 8-ounce glasses

6 medium-size cooking apples,
about 2 pounds
½ cup water
2 lemons, rind and juice
4 cups sugar

METHOD:
1. Core apples, and chop. Place apples, water, and lemon rind in a heavy kettle.
2. Heat to boiling. Simmer until apples are soft, about 30 minutes. Place in a jelly bag, and drain overnight.
3. The next day, add lemon juice and sugar to apple juice in the same kettle. Heat to boiling. Boil until jelly tests for set, about 30 minutes. Seal in hot sterilized glasses.

NOTE:
To make a lovely glaze for a fruit tart, melt this jelly and spread over the fruit. Or eat it with cheese and crackers as a light dessert.

Apple Jelly, Grape Jelly, and Red Cherry Jam are three American favorites that taste best when preserved at home.

Apple-Orange Jam

Cooking time: 30 minutes

Yield: 5 8-ounce glasses

- 6 medium-size cooking apples, about 2 pounds
- 3 oranges, rind and juice
- 1 cup water
- 4½ cups sugar

METHOD:
1. Peel, core, and slice apples as for pie.
2. Combine apples, orange rind, and water in a heavy kettle.
3. Heat to boiling. Simmer, stirring often, until soft.
4. Add sugar and orange juice, and stir until sugar dissolves.
5. Boil rapidly until jam sets, about 25 minutes.
6. Allow jam to cool slightly. Seal in hot sterilized glasses.

NOTE:
This jam is particularly good on hot corn bread or bran muffins.

Apple-Orange Jelly

Cooking time: 1 hour

Yield: 5 8-ounce glasses

- 6 medium-size cooking apples, about 2 pounds
- ½ cup water
- 2 oranges, rind and juice
- 4 cups sugar

METHOD:
1. Chop apples. Place apples, water, and orange rind in a heavy kettle.
2. Heat to boiling. Simmer until apples are soft, about 30 minutes. Place in a jelly bag, and drain overnight.
3. The next day, add orange juice and sugar to apple juice in the same kettle. Heat to

boiling. Boil until jelly tests for set, about 30 minutes. Seal in hot sterilized glasses.

NOTE:
Ever try mixing peanut butter and jelly together? It makes a very nice sandwich spread. Use your blender to get a smooth spread. Children will love Apple-Orange Jelly this way.

Apple-Peach Jam

Cooking time: 20 minutes

Yield: 3 8-ounce glasses

- 2 medium-size tart green apples, about 12 ounces
- 4 medium-size firm peaches, peeled and sliced, about 1 pound
- 2 lemons, juice of
- 3 cups sugar

METHOD:
1. Core unpeeled apples, and slice as for pie. Tie cores in a piece of cheesecloth.
2. Combine apples with peaches, lemon juice, and sugar in a heavy kettle.
3. Heat to boiling. Simmer, stirring often, until apples are transparent, about 20 minutes. Remove apple-core bag.
4. Allow jam to cool slightly, then stir. Seal in hot sterilized glasses.

NOTE:
This is a lovely recipe to start the summer preserving season.

Apple-Pineapple Jam

Cooking time: 35 minutes

Yield: 6 8-ounce glasses

  1 large ripe pineapple
  3 medium-size cooking apples, peeled,
     cored, and diced, about 1 pound
  ¼ cup water
  4 cups sugar

METHOD:
1. Slice, peel, core, and cube pineapple.
2. Combine with diced apples and water in a heavy kettle.
3. Heat to boiling. Simmer, stirring often, until fruits are soft. Add sugar and stir until sugar dissolves.
4. Boil rapidly until jam sets, about 30 minutes. Allow jam to cool slightly, then stir to distribute fruits. Seal in hot sterilized glasses.

NOTE:
Nice with cottage cheese or yogurt.

Apple-Plum Jam

Cooking time: 30 minutes

Yield: 8 8-ounce glasses

  3 medium-size cooking apples,
     about 1 pound
 12 ripe Damson plums, pitted and sliced,
     about 2 pounds
  ½ cup water
  6 cups sugar

METHOD:
1. Peel, core, and slice apples.
2. Combine apples, plums, and water in a heavy kettle.
3. Heat to boiling. Simmer, stirring often, until fruits are soft. Add sugar, and stir until sugar dissolves.
4. Boil until jam sets, about 30 minutes. Seal in hot sterilized glasses.

NOTE:
Spark up your breakfast with this jam. Spread on French toast and sprinkle with powdered sugar.

Apple-Rhubarb Jam

Cooking time: 30 minutes

Yield: 6 8-ounce glasses

  3 medium-size cooking apples,
     about 1 pound
  3 cups rhubarb, about 1 pound
  ¼ cup water
  4 cups sugar

METHOD:

1. Peel, core, and dice applies; dice rhubarb.
2. Combine apples with rhubarb, water, and sugar in a heavy kettle.
3. Heat to boiling. Simmer, stirring often, until sugar dissolves and fruits are soft.
4. Boil rapidly until jam sets, about 30 minutes. Seal in hot sterilized glasses.

NOTE:

If fresh rhubarb is unobtainable, use a pound of frozen. Do not thaw, just add to the apples and continue to cook as per recipe.

Apricot Jam

Cooking time: 30 minutes

Yield: 3 8-ounce glasses

12 ripe apricots, about 1 pound
 3 tablespoons water
 2 cups sugar
 ½ lemon, juice of
        or
 ¼ teaspoon citric acid

METHOD:

1. Halve, pit, and slice apricots. Tie apricot pits in a piece of cheesecloth.
2. Combine apricots, pit bag, and water in a heavy kettle.
3. Heat to boiling. Simmer, stirring often, until apricots are soft. Add sugar and lemon juice, and stir until sugar dissolves. Remove pit bag.
4. Boil rapidly until jam sets, about 10 minutes. Seal in hot sterilized glasses.

NOTE:

With apricot jam, you bring summer flavor to your family's breakfast table the year around.

Dried Apricot Jam

Cooking time: 1 hour 15 minutes

Yield: 4 8-ounce glasses

 3 cups dried apricots, about 1 pound
 6 cups water
 4 cups sugar
 2 lemons, juice of

METHOD:

1. Combine dried apricots and water in a large glass or china bowl. Cover bowl. Allow to stand 2 days.
2. When ready to cook, place apricots and water in a heavy kettle.
3. Heat to boiling. Simmer until apricots soften. Add sugar and lemon juice, and stir until sugar dissolves.
4. Boil rapidly until set, about 1 hour, skimming if necessary. Seal in hot sterilized glasses.

NOTE:

Try adding ¼ cup slivered almonds or macadamia nuts to this jam. Stir into jam after cooking. When making coffee cake or muffins, add jam to dough, or use as a glaze on cake or muffins.

Low Calorie Apricot Jam

Cooking time: 45 minutes

Yield: 6 8-ounce glasses

    36 ripe apricots, about 3 pounds
    ½ cup water
    46 saccharin tablets
     4 cups glycerine*

METHOD:
1. Peel apricots. Place in a heavy kettle with water.
2. Heat to boiling. Cook, stirring several times, until fruit softens, about 40 minutes. Remove pits with a slotted spoon.
3. Remove ½ cup hot liquid from kettle. Dissolve saccharin tablets in hot liquid. Stir into kettle with glycerine.
4. Cook until jam thickens, about 5 minutes. Seal in hot sterilized glasses.

NOTE:
This will be a delightful surprise to serve to guests who are watching their waistlines.

*Glycerine used in low-calorie recipes may be purchased from a drugstore. Ask your druggist for commercial glycerine, the type most suitable for your jam.

Apricot-Apple Jam

Cooking time: 15 minutes

Yield: 8–9 8-ounce glasses

    1 can (1 pound 13 ounces) apricot halves
  3–4 cooking apples, peeled, cored, and
       sliced, about 1 pound
    7 cups sugar
    1 lemon, juice of
    1 bottle (6 ounces) liquid pectin

METHOD:
1. Drain juice from the apricots into a kettle. Add apples and cook until soft.
2. Add the cut-up apricots, sugar, and lemon juice.

3. Cook and stir over moderate heat until sugar is completely dissolved.
4. Bring to a fast rolling boil, and boil rapidly for 2 minutes.
5. Stir in pectin and immediately remove from heat.
6. Continue stirring for about 5 minutes to keep fruit distributed in syrup. Skim.
7. Seal in hot sterilized glasses.

NOTE:
I make this jam in the winter when most fresh fruits are scarce. A good addition to hot muffins and crisp bacon.

Apricot-Cherry Jam

Cooking time: 30 minutes

Yield: 7 8-ounce glasses

    24 ripe apricots, about 2 pounds
     4 cups sour cherries, about 1 pound
    ¼ cup water
     6 cups sugar
     2 lemons, juice of

METHOD:
1. Halve, pit, and slice apricots.
2. Combine apricots with cherries and water in a heavy kettle.
3. Heat to boiling. Simmer, stirring often, until cherry pits rise to the top. Remove pits with a slotted spoon. Continue cooking until fruits are soft.
4. Add sugar and lemon juice, and stir until sugar dissolves.
5. Boil rapidly, stirring often, until jam sets, about 10 minutes. Seal in hot sterilized glasses.

NOTE:
This jam mixes nicely with plain yogurt. Or spread thinly on crêpes for an elegant party dessert.

Apricot-Pear Jam

Cooking time: 1 hour

Yield: 9 8-ounce glasses

15 firm, not-too-ripe, pears, about 5 pounds
3 cups dried apricots, about 1 pound
1 cup water
9 cups sugar

METHOD:

1. Peel, core, and cut pears in 1-inch pieces. Put pears and apricots through a food chopper, using a medium blade.
2. Place prepared fruits in a heavy kettle with water.
3. Heat to boiling. Add sugar gradually, stirring until sugar dissolves.
4. Continue cooking until fruit is transparent and jam is thick, about 1 hour. Seal in hot sterilized glasses.

NOTE:

Lovely with hot buttered rolls.

Banana-Lemon Jam

Cooking time: 1 hour

Yield: 3 8-ounce glasses

6 large ripe bananas, about 2 pounds
3 lemons, juice and rind
2 cups superfine sugar

METHOD:

1. Peel bananas and dice. Combine bananas, lemon juice, and rind in a large china or glass bowl. Sprinkle bananas with sugar.
2. Cover bowl, and allow to stand until sugar dissolves, about 1 hour. Place mixture in a heavy kettle.
3. Heat slowly to boiling. Simmer, stirring and skimming often, until jam tests for set, about 1 hour. Seal in hot sterilized glasses.
4. Refrigerate jam.

NOTE:

Banana jams should be refrigerated, so if you are giving as a gift or selling at a bazaar, be sure to write "refrigerate" on labels.

Banana-Orange Jam

Cooking time: 1 hour 15 minutes

Yield: 3 8-ounce glasses

6 large ripe bananas, about 2 pounds
3 oranges, juice and rind
2 cups superfine sugar

METHOD:

1. Peel bananas and cut into thin slices. Place in a heavy kettle with orange juice and rind. Sprinkle with sugar. Allow to stand for 30 minutes.
2. Heat slowly to boiling. Simmer, stirring and skimming often, until jam tests for set, about 1 hour 15 minutes. Seal in hot sterilized glasses.
3. Refrigerate jam.

NOTE:

The flavor and color of this jam will vary with the ripeness of banana used. Bananas when fully ripe will develop a speckled brown skin. They are then at their best in flavor.

Banana-Peach Jam

Cooking time: 10 minutes

Yield: 7 8-ounce glasses

4 firm yellow bananas, about 1 pound
4 large ripe peaches, about 1 pound
7 cups sugar
¼ cup lemon juice
½ bottle (3 ounces) liquid pectin

METHOD:
1. Peel fruits, discard pits. Mash to a pulp.
2. Combine fruit pulp, sugar, and lemon juice. Stir over very low heat until sugar dissolves.
3. Bring to a full rolling boil. Cook 3 minutes, stirring constantly.
4. Remove from heat, and stir in pectin. Stir 5 minutes to keep fruit well distributed.
5. Skim and seal in hot sterilized glasses and refrigerate.

NOTE:
Spread cooked sweet potatoes or yams in a baking dish, dot generously with Banana-Peach Jam, drizzle on melted butter, broil to a bubbling brown. Serve with pork chops or baked ham slice.

Banana-Pineapple Jam

Cooking time: 10 minutes

Yield: 8–9 8-ounce glasses

5 large yellow ripe bananas, about 1½ pounds
1 can (1 pound 13 ounces) crushed or cubed pineapple, drained
6½ cups sugar
1 bottle (6 ounces) liquid pectin

METHOD:
1. Peel the bananas, then mash with the pineapple and sugar.

2. Stir over low heat until sugar dissolves. Bring to a boil.
3. Boil mixture for 1 minute. Remove from heat, stir in pectin, and stir 5 minutes.
4. Skim and seal in hot sterilized glasses. Refrigerate.

NOTE:
Try this luxurious jam with slices of pound cake; top with whipped cream.

Beet-Apple Jam

Cooking time: 3 hours

Yield: 6 8-ounce glasses

4 medium-size beets, about 1 pound
6 medium-size green apples, about 2 pounds
1 cup sugar
½ teaspoon salt
water

METHOD:
1. Boil the beets until tender, about 1 hour. Peel and dice beets. Peel, core, and dice apples.
2. Place beets, apples, sugar, and salt in a heavy kettle. Cover with water.
3. Heat to boiling. Simmer until syrupy, about 2 hours. Seal in hot sterilized glasses.

NOTE:
Good with hamburgers, cold-meat sandwiches, and with cheese and crackers.

Blackberry Jam

Cooking time: 25 minutes

Yield: 3 8-ounce glasses

6 cups blackberries, 2 pounds
1 lemon, juice of
sugar

METHOD:
1. Combine blackberries and lemon juice in a heavy kettle.
2. Heat to boiling. Simmer until blackberries are soft, about 15 minutes. Press through a sieve to remove seeds.
3. Measure fruit and add 2 cups of sugar for every 2 cups of fruit in same kettle.
4. Boil until jam sets, about 10 minutes. Seal in hot sterilized glasses.

NOTE:
If you like the flavor of blackberries but hate the seeds, this jam is for you. Put a dollop of Blackberry Jam on tapioca pudding.

Blackberry Jelly

Cooking time: 25 minutes

Yield: 3 8-ounce glasses

1 medium-size apple
or
1 lemon
4 cups ripe blackberries
¼ cup water
3 cups sugar

METHOD:
1. Chop apple or cut lemon into thin slices. Combine with blackberries in a heavy kettle with water.
2. Heat to boiling. Simmer until berries are soft, about 15 minutes. Place in a jelly bag, and drain overnight.
3. The next day, add sugar, and stir until sugar dissolves.
4. Boil rapidly until jelly tests for set, about 10 minutes. Seal in hot sterilized glasses.

NOTE:
To spice Blackberry Jelly, add 1 teaspoon allspice. Serve with cold-meat platters for summer suppers.

Blackberry-Apple Jam

Cooking time: 25 minutes

Yield: 9 8-ounce glasses

3 medium-size cooking apples,
about 1 pound
¼ cup water
3 cups blackberries, about 1 pound
4 cups sugar

METHOD:
1. Peel, core, and slice apples, as for pie.
2. Combine apple slices and water in a heavy kettle.
3. Heat to boiling. Simmer, stirring often, until soft. Add blackberries, and continue cooking until berries are soft. Add sugar, and stir until sugar dissolves.
4. Boil rapidly until jam sets, about 10 minutes. Seal in hot sterilized glasses.

NOTE:
Take some bread straight from the oven, spread it with this jam, and you have a feast for the gods.

Blackberry-Pineapple-Apple Jam

Cooking time: 25 minutes

Yield: 9 8-ounce glasses

 1 large pineapple
 2 large cooking apples, about 1 pound
 ¼ cup water
 3 cups blackberries, 1 pound
 6 cups sugar
 3 lemons, juice of

METHOD:
1. Slice, peel, core, and dice pineapple. Peel, core, and slice apples.
2. Combine pineapple, apple, and water in a heavy kettle.
3. Heat to boiling. Simmer, stirring often, 10 minutes. Add blackberries. Continue cooking 10 minutes, or until fruits are soft.
4. Stir in sugar and lemon juice until sugar dissolves.
5. Boil rapidly until jam sets, about 5 minutes. Seal in hot sterilized glasses.

NOTE:
A triple treat from three favorite fruits.

Blueberry Jam

Cooking time: 10 minutes

Yield: 6 8-ounce glasses

 6 cups blueberries, 3 pints
 1 lemon, rind and juice
 7 cups sugar

METHOD:
1. Combine blueberries, lemon rind and juice, and sugar.
2. Heat *very slowly* to a boil, mashing some of the berries with the back of a wooden spoon to make more juice.
3. Boil rapidly until jam tests for set, about 5 minutes. Seal in hot sterilized glasses.

NOTE:
Blueberry Jam is a delicious topping for vanilla ice cream. For breakfast spread it on French toast.

Blueberry-Apple Jam

Cooking time: 20 minutes

Yield: 8 8-ounce glasses

 6 cups sugar
 ½ cup water
 2 teaspoons lemon juice
 4 cups blueberries, 2 pints
 3 large apples, peeled, cored, and chopped, 1 pound

METHOD:
1. Combine sugar, water, and lemon juice in a heavy kettle.
2. Heat to boiling. Stir in blueberries and chopped apple. Cook, stirring constantly, until jam tests for set, about 15 minutes. Seal in hot sterilized glasses.

NOTE:
When winter winds blow around your house, bring out a jar of this jam to treat the family at breakfast. Nice with pancakes or waffles.

Children of all ages love peanut butter sandwiches with jelly or jam. For a Halloween party for the kids or a grown-up get-together before the football game, put out bread and peanut butter and a selection of your own preserves. Pictured clockwise: Guava Jelly, Red Currant Jelly, Blackberry Jam, Plum-Raspberry Jam, Pineapple-Apricot Jam, Bing Cherry Jam.

Carrot Jam

Cooking time: 50 minutes

Yield: 9 8-ounce glasses

12 large carrots, 3 pounds
    water
12 cups sugar
 6 lemons, juice and rind
 6 tablespoons brandy
 1 tablespoon almonds,
    blanched and slivered

METHOD:

1. Peel and slice carrots. Place in a heavy kettle. Add just enough water to cover bottom of kettle.
2. Heat to boiling. Cook until soft. Whirl in blender or press through sieve. (Measure—you should have 12 cups.)
3. Combine carrot puree with sugar and lemon juice and rind in same kettle, stirring until sugar dissolves.
4. Heat to boiling. Boil rapidly until jam tests for set, about 50 minutes.
5. Add brandy and almonds, stirring well. Seal in hot sterilized glasses.

NOTE:

A good jam to make when fruit is scarce.

Carrot-Lemon Jam

Cooking time: 2 hours

Yield: 7 8-ounce glasses

12 large carrots, about 3 pounds
12 cups sugar
 3 oranges, juice and rind
 1 lemon, juice and rind
 ⅛ teaspoon salt

METHOD:

1. Peel carrots and coarsely grate. (Measure—you should have 12 cups.) Combine with sugar in a heavy kettle. Cover kettle and allow to stand overnight.
2. Add orange and lemon rinds and juices and salt to kettle.
3. Heat to boiling. Simmer, stirring and skimming often, until jam tests for set, about 2 hours. Seal in hot sterilized glasses.

NOTE:

Makes nice sandwiches for hungry youngsters, even those who hate carrots.

Bing Cherry Jam

Cooking time: 30 minutes

Yield: 3 8-ounce glasses

5 cups Bing cherries, about 1¼ pounds
2 cups sugar
1 lemon, juice of

METHOD:

1. Stem and pit cherries. Place in a large glass or china bowl. Sprinkle with sugar. Cover bowl with a towel and allow to stand for several hours.
2. Place cherry mixture in a heavy kettle. Add lemon juice and stir until sugar dissolves.
3. Heat to boiling. Boil rapidly until syrup is fairly firm, about 30 minutes. Seal in hot sterilized glasses.

NOTE:

Cherries are divided into two groups: sweet and sour. Sweet cherries are usually called Bing, and have flesh ranging from deep mahogany to black. They are larger than sour cherries, heart-shaped and firm, yet tender. They are often eaten uncooked.

Bing Cherry Jam should never be stiff. Use in small tarts, in thin pancakes, or as a topping for ice cream.

Bing Cherry-Gooseberry Jam

Cooking time: 30 minutes

Yield: 6 8-ounce glasses

6 cups Bing cherries, about 2 pounds
6 cups gooseberries, about 2 pounds
water
8 cups sugar

METHOD:

1. Pit cherries. Place cherries and gooseberries in a heavy kettle with enough water just to cover. Heat to boiling. Cook the fruit until soft, about 15 minutes.
2. Add sugar to kettle. Cook, stirring often, until mixture thickens, about 15 minutes. Seal in hot sterilized glasses.

NOTE:

This rich-looking jam goes well with thick slices of toasted French bread.

Ground Cherry Jam

Cooking time: 40 minutes

Yield: 8 8-ounce glasses

6 cups ground cherries
(husked), about 1½ pounds
1 cup water
8 cups sugar
2 lemons, juice of
1½ cups light corn syrup

METHOD:

1. Combine husked ground cherries and water in a heavy kettle.
2. Heat to boiling. Simmer for 10 minutes. Add sugar, lemon juice, and corn syrup. Simmer 30 minutes. Allow to stand overnight.
3. The next day, heat jam to boiling. Seal in hot sterilized glasses.

NOTE:

Ground cherries, also known as husk tomatoes, are a fruit found mostly in the Middle West and North Atlantic states during the fall. They resemble miniature Chinese lanterns.

Ground Cherry Jam makes a thin but delicious jam. For a thicker product, allow the second-boiled jam to stand another day, then bring to a boil a third time, and seal in hot sterilized glasses. Perfect with hot buttered corn bread.

Red Cherry Jam

Cooking time: 20 minutes

Yield: 8 8-ounce glasses

- 10 cups sour red cherries, pitted, 2½ pounds
- ½ cup water
- 1 lemon, juice of
- 6 cups sugar
- 1 bottle (6 ounces) liquid pectin
- ¼ teaspoon almond extract

METHOD:
1. Combine cherries, water, and lemon juice, cover and simmer for 10–12 minutes.
2. Stir in sugar, and heat until sugar dissolves. Stir often to prevent scorching.
3. Bring to a full rolling boil, and boil rapidly for 3 minutes.
4. Stir in the pectin. Continue to cook for 1 minute.
5. Remove from heat, skim. Add almond extract. Allow to cool, stirring frequently.
6. Seal in hot sterilized glasses.

NOTE:
Sour cherries range in color from red to nearly black. Rounder and softer-textured than sweet cherries, they are also hardier. Sour cherries are used cooked.

Spread Red Cherry Jam on bakery-bought cheesecake for flavor and color.

Red Cherry-Apricot Jam

Cooking time: 45 minutes

Yield: 6 8-ounce glasses

- 8 cups sour red cherries, 2 pounds
- 24 ripe apricots, 2 pounds
- ½ cup water
- 8 cups sugar
- 4 lemons, juice of

METHOD:
1. Stem and pit cherries. Pit and quarter apricots. Tie pits in a piece of cheesecloth. Combine cherries, apricots, water, and bag in a heavy kettle.
2. Heat slowly, stirring often, until cherries are soft, about 20 minutes. Add sugar and lemon juice, stirring until sugar dissolves.
3. Boil rapidly until jam tests for set, about 25 minutes. Remove bag with pits. Seal in hot sterilized glasses.

NOTE:
Save Cherry-Apricot Jam for special occasions and serve with freshly made popovers.

Swiss Style Cherry Jam

Cooking time: 40 minutes
                    Yield: 12 8-ounce glasses

6 cups red currants, stemmed
    cold water
16 cups Bing cherries, 4 pounds
7½ cups sugar

METHOD:

1. Place currants in a heavy kettle, and just cover with cold water.
2. Heat slowly until currants are soft. Press currants through a fine sieve or jelly bag.
3. Stem and pit cherries. Tie pits in a piece of cheesecloth.
4. Return currant juice to kettle with sugar. Cook, stirring often, until sugar dissolves.
5. Add cherries and bag with pits. Cook slowly until liquid is of a syrupy consistency, about 20 minutes. Remove bag with pits. Seal in hot sterilized glasses.

NOTE:

This jam should never be stiff and is excellent for cherry tartlets. In a glass dish, place a peach half and a scoop of vanilla ice cream, and pour over some of this jam. *Voilà*! a delightful dessert made in a few minutes.

Chestnut Jam

Cooking time: 40 minutes
                    Yield: 4 8-ounce glasses

8 cups fresh chestnuts, 2 pounds
    cold water
3 cups sugar
1 cup water
3 teaspoons vanilla extract

METHOD:

1. Cut a cross on both ends of each chestnut. (A cross cut in the chestnut shell expands in boiling water, thus making it easier to remove the shell later.) Place in a heavy kettle and cover with cold water.
2. Heat to boiling. Simmer 20 minutes, or until nuts are tender. Drain and cool nuts. Peel off skins and whirl in blender or press through sieve to make a puree.
3. Combine sugar, 1 cup water, and vanilla in the same kettle. Heat to boiling. Boil to make a syrup, about 10 minutes. Add chestnut puree. Cook slowly, stirring constantly, until mixture thickens, about 10 minutes. Seal in hot sterilized glasses.

NOTE:

This is a lovely filling to use when making a Swedish coffee ring for brunch or miniature tarts for a luncheon buffet.

Cranberry Jam

Cooking time: 35 minutes

Yield: 8–10 8-ounce glasses

8 cups fresh cranberries, 2 pounds
1 cup water
3 cups sugar

METHOD:

1. Combine cranberries and water in a heavy kettle.
2. Heat to boiling. Simmer until cranberries are soft. Add sugar, and stir until sugar dissolves.
3. Boil rapidly until jam tests for set, about 15 minutes. Seal in hot sterilized glasses.

NOTE:

For variety, add the grated rind of 2 oranges and 1 cup raisins to the berries while cooking. When setting point is reached, in 20–35 minutes, add 1 cup blanched, chopped almonds. This should be served with turkey, roast pork, or cold meats.

Cranberry Jelly

Cooking time: 30 minutes

Yield: 5 8-ounce glasses

8 cups fresh cranberries, 2 pounds
2 large oranges
1½ cups water
5 cups sugar

METHOD:

1. Stem cranberries. Halve, seed, and thinly slice oranges. Combine cranberries, oranges, and water in a heavy kettle.
2. Heat to boiling. Cook until berries are soft, about 20 minutes. Place in a jelly bag, and drain overnight.
3. The next day, combine juice and sugar in the same kettle. Heat to boiling, stirring until sugar dissolves. Boil until jelly tests for set, about 10 minutes. Seal in hot sterilized glasses.

NOTE:

Of course, this goes with your Thanksgiving or Christmas turkey! But it is also excellent with roast chicken for everyday meals.

Cranberry-Grape Jelly

Cooking time: 30 minutes

Yield: 7 8-ounce glasses

**8 cups fresh cranberries, stemmed,
2 pounds**
**4 cups grapes (white, if possible),
stemmed, 2 pounds**
1 cup water
7 cups sugar
2 lemons, juice of

METHOD:
1. Combine cranberries with grapes and water in a heavy kettle.
2. Heat to boiling. Cook until berries are tender, about 20 minutes. Place in a jelly bag, and drain overnight.
3. The next day, combine berry juices, sugar, and lemon juice in the same kettle. Heat to boiling, stirring until sugar dissolves. Boil until jelly tests for set, about 10 minutes. Seal in hot sterilized glasses.

NOTE:
A special treat with holiday turkey, duck, goose, or baked fresh ham.

Cucumber Jam

Cooking time: 25 minutes

Yield: 3 8-ounce glasses

4 large cucumbers
½ cup water
4 cups sugar
2 lemons, juice of

METHOD:
1. Peel and dice cucumber. Combine cucumber and water in a heavy kettle. Add sugar and lemon juice, stirring until sugar dissolves.
2. Heat to boiling. Boil rapidly until jam tests for set, about 25 minutes. Seal in hot sterilized glasses.

NOTE:
This jam is pale in color, so you may want to add a few drops of green food coloring. As a variation, I sometimes add a little powdered ginger (¼–½ teaspoon). Thin crackers spread with cream cheese and a dab of cucumber jam makes a nice snack.

Cucumber Jelly

Cooking time: 30 minutes

Yield: 3 8-ounce glasses

8 large cucumbers, about 4 pounds
¼ cup water
2 cups sugar
1 lemon, juice of
¼ teaspoon ground ginger
green food coloring (optional)

METHOD:
1. Remove cucumber ends and discard. Cut cucumber into thin slices. Combine with water in a heavy kettle.

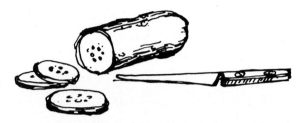

Bar-le-Duc Currant Jam

Cooking time: 10 minutes

Yield: 12 8-ounce glasses

18 cups black or red currants, stemmed, about 6 pounds
6 cups sugar
½ cup honey

METHOD:
1. Place 6 cups of the currants in a heavy kettle.
2. Heat over low heat, crushing berries to make some juice. Add remaining currants.
3. Heat to boiling. Simmer 1 minute. Stir in sugar, and simmer, stirring often, for 5 minutes.
4. Add honey. Simmer 4 minutes longer. Seal in hot sterilized glasses.

NOTE:
Bar-le-Duc is a town in Lorraine, France, which is famous for its currants and grapes. For a different breakfast dish, spread pancakes with Bar-le-Duc Currant Jam and sour cream; stack pancakes three at a time and you'll make a hit!

2. Heat to boiling. Simmer until a soft pulp is formed, mashing with a wooden spoon to extract as much juice as possible, about 20 minutes. Place in a jelly bag, and drain overnight.
3. The next day, combine cucumber juice, sugar, lemon juice, and ginger in the same kettle. Stir until sugar dissolves. Heat to boiling. Boil until jelly tests for set, about 10 minutes. Add a few drops of green food coloring, if you wish. Seal in hot sterilized glasses.

NOTE:
Serve Cucumber Jelly with yogurt. Goes well with shrimps or salmon sandwiches. Nice on thin crackers.

Black Currant Jam

Cooking time: 40 minutes

Yield: 3 8-ounce glasses

  3 **cups black currants, stemmed (or red, if black currants are unobtainable), about 1 pound**
1½ **cups water**
2½ **cups sugar**

METHOD:

1. Combine currants with water in a heavy kettle.
2. Heat to boiling. Simmer slowly, stirring often, until very soft. Test skins. (They should be mushy when rubbed between the fingers.) Add sugar, and stir until sugar dissolves.
3. Boil rapidly, stirring often, just until jam sets, about 10 minutes. Seal in hot sterilized glasses.

NOTE:

Serve with piping hot biscuits.

Black and Red Currant Jam, Number I

Cooking time: 40 minutes

Yield: 7 8-ounce glasses

  3 **cups black currants, stemmed, about 1 pound**
  3 **cups red currants, stemmed, about 1 pound**
1½ **cups water**
4½ **cups sugar**

METHOD:

1. Combine black and red currants with water in a heavy kettle.
2. Heat to boiling. Simmer, stirring often, until very soft, when skins are tested. Add sugar and stir until sugar dissolves.
3. Boil rapidly, stirring often, just until jam sets, about 10 minutes. Seal in hot sterilized glasses.

NOTE:

Keep Black and Red Currant Jam on the shelf to bring back memories of summer days.

Black and Red Currant Jam, Number II

Cooking time: 30 minutes

Yield: 9 8-ounce glasses

  6 cups black currants, stemmed, about 2 pounds
2½ cups water
  3 cups red currants, stemmed, about 1 pound
  6 cups sugar

METHOD:

1. Combine black currants and water in a heavy kettle.
2. Heat to boiling. Simmer, stirring often, 10 minutes. Add red currants. Simmer 10 minutes longer, until soft when skins are tested. Add sugar, and stir until sugar dissolves.
3. Boil just until jam is set, about 10 minutes. Seal in hot sterilized glasses.

NOTE:

Try with salted crackers and cheese for a light and elegant dessert.

Black Currant-Apple Jam

Cooking time: 45 minutes

Yield: 5 8-ounce glasses

  3 cups black currants, stemmed, about 1 pound
  1 cup water
  3 medium-size cooking apples, peeled, cored, and sliced
4½ cups sugar

METHOD:

1. Combine currants and water in a heavy kettle.
2. Heat to boiling. Simmer, stirring often, until very soft, when skins are tested. Add sliced apples. Cook until apples are soft, about 15 minutes. Stir in sugar, and stir until sugar dissolves.
3. Boil rapidly until jam sets, about 10 minutes. Seal in hot sterilized glasses.

NOTE:

Black Currant-Apple Jam is a good choice when red currants are expensive or scarce.

Black Currant-Pineapple Jam

Cooking time: 12 minutes

Yield: 6–7 8-ounce glasses

  3 cans (1 pound each) black currants
      or
  3 pounds frozen black currants
  1 can (1 pound) pineapple tidbits, drained
  1 orange, rind and juice
  4 cups sugar
½ bottle (3 ounces) liquid pectin

METHOD:

1. Combine currants, pineapple, orange rind and juice, and sugar in a heavy kettle.
2. Bring to a full rolling boil. Boil rapidly for 2 minutes.
3. Stir in pectin, and remove from heat. Stir for about 5 minutes to keep fruit distributed. Skim. Seal in hot sterilized glasses.

NOTE:

This is a treat that starts with canned fruits from your pantry shelf. Serve over silver-dollar pancakes for a special brunch.

Red Currant Jelly

Cooking time: 40 minutes

Yield: 6 8-ounce glasses

6 cups red currants, stemmed (or black,
   if red currants are unobtainable),
   about 2 pounds
2 cups water
6 cups sugar

METHOD:
1. Combine currants and water in a heavy kettle.
2. Heat to boiling. Simmer until currants are soft, about 20 minutes. Place in a jelly bag, and drain overnight.
3. The next day, heat juice to boiling in the same kettle. Add sugar, and stir until sugar dissolves. Boil until jelly tests for set, about 20 minutes. Seal in hot sterilized glasses.

NOTE:
If you like a spiced flavor, add 1 level teaspoon pumpkin-pie spice to the sugar. Serve Red Currant Jelly with cheese omelets, hot biscuits, and popovers, or with rabbit, roast lamb, pork, etc.

Date Jam

Cooking time: 1 hour

Yield: 10 8-ounce glasses

6 cups fresh dates, pitted, 3 pounds
24 large carrots, grated, 4 pounds
6 cups sugar
3 cups water
½ cup almonds, blanched and slivered

METHOD:
1. Combine dates, carrots, sugar, water, and almonds in a heavy kettle. Stir until sugar dissolves.
2. Heat to boiling. Simmer, stirring and skimming often, until jam tests for set, about 1 hour. Seal in hot sterilized glasses.

NOTE:
Try spreading this jam on brown bread with a layer of cream cheese.

Fig Jam

Cooking time: 45 minutes

Yield: 12 8-ounce glasses

14 cups fresh figs, 7 pounds
9 pounds sugar
1 can (1 pound and 13 ounces) crushed
   pineapple
3 lemons, juice and rind
1 tablespoon ground cloves
1 tablespoon ground allspice
1 tablespoon ground cinnamon

METHOD:
1. Peel and mash figs. Combine with sugar, crushed pineapple, lemon juice and rind, and spice in a heavy kettle. Stir until sugar dissolves.

2. Heal to boiling. Simmer, stirring often, until thick and jam tests for set, about 45 minutes.
3. Allow to cool, then stir to distribute fruit. Seal in hot sterilized glasses.

NOTE:

Try this as a filling for bar cookies and dessert tarts.

Fig-Lemon Jam

Cooking time: 1 hour

Yield: 7 8-ounce glasses

  4 cups dried figs, 2 pounds
  4 cups cold water
  6 cups sugar
  4 lemons, juice and rind

METHOD:

1. Cut figs into small pieces. Combine with cold water in a heavy kettle. Cover kettle and allow to soak overnight.
2. The next day, add sugar, and stir until sugar dissolves.
3. Heat to boiling, and skim. Add lemon juice and rind. Simmer, stirring and skimming often, until jam tests for set, about 1 hour. Cool. Seal in hot sterilized glasses.

NOTE:

This jam will go perfectly with a roast of pork or a rolled veal shoulder.

Fruit Medley

Cooking time: 30 minutes

Yield: 8 8-ounce glasses

  6 cups sour red cherries, 1½ pounds
18 fresh apricots, 1½ pounds
      or
  6 medium-size peaches, 1½ pounds
  4 cups fresh red raspberries, 1 pound
      or
  4 cups frozen raspberries
  7 cups sugar

METHOD:

1. Stem and pit cherries. Quarter and pit apricots, or peel, halve, pit, and slice peaches. Tie fruit pits in a piece of cheesecloth.
2. Combine prepared fruits with raspberries in a heavy kettle. Add sugar and bag with pits, and stir until sugar dissolves.
3. Heat quickly to boiling, stirring often. Boil rapidly until fruits are clear and tender and test for set, about 30 minutes.
4. Remove bag with pits. Allow to cool. Seal in hot sterilized glasses.

NOTE:

A gala gathering of fruits such as this deserves giving as a gift or selling at a bazaar.

Gooseberry Jam

Cooking time: 15 minutes

Yield: 4 8-ounce glasses

**4 cups green or pink gooseberries,
 about 2 pounds
½ lemon, juice and rind
½ cup water
4 cups sugar**

METHOD:
1. Pick over and stem berries.
2. Combine all ingredients in heavy kettle and mix well.
3. Cook and stir over moderate heat, mashing berries with a wooden spoon, until sugar is completely dissolved.
4. Bring mixture to a rapid boil.
5. Lower heat and cook mixture about 15 minutes, or until thick, stirring continuously.
6. Pour into hot sterilized glasses. Let cool before sealing.

NOTE:
The gooseberry season is very short, so make this recipe as soon as you see berries on the bush or in the market.

Low Calorie Gooseberry Jam

Cooking time: 25 minutes

Yield: 5 8-ounce glasses

**9 cups green or pink gooseberries,
 about 3 pounds
½ cup water
48 saccharin tablets
4 cups glycerine**

METHOD:
1. Stem gooseberries, and place with water in a heavy kettle.
2. Heat to boiling. Cook, stirring several times, until fruit softens, about 20 minutes.

3. Remove ½ cup hot liquid from kettle. Dissolve saccharin tablets in hot liquid. Stir into kettle with glycerine.
4. Cook until jam thickens, about 5 minutes. Seal in hot sterilized glasses.

NOTE:
The season for gooseberries is short, so put them up when first you see them in the market.

Grape Jelly

Cooking time: 25 minutes

Yield: 8 8-ounce glasses

**6 cups ripe black grapes, stemmed,
 3 pounds
½ cup water
6½ cups sugar
2 tablespoons lemon juice
1 bottle (6 ounces) liquid pectin**

METHOD:
1. Place grapes and water in a heavy kettle. Mash grapes with a wooden spoon to extract juice.
2. Heat to boiling. Cover kettle. Simmer 10 minutes. Place in a jelly bag, and drain overnight.
3. Combine grape juice, sugar, and lemon juice in the same kettle. Bring to a full rolling boil, cook 1 minute, stirring constantly.
4. Remove from heat, and stir in pectin. Stir 5 minutes. Skim. Seal in hot sterilized glasses.

NOTE:
This is the perfect touch for a breakfast tray with golden biscuits and sweet butter.

Concord Grape Jelly

Cooking time: 35 minutes

Yield: 5 8-ounce glasses

10 cups ripe Concord grapes, stemmed, about 5 pounds

4⅓ cups sugar

METHOD:

1. Place grapes in a heavy kettle.
2. Cook over a *very low* heat, mashing and pressing with a wooden spoon to extract as much juice as possible.
3. Strain grapes through a piece of cheesecloth. Return juice to same kettle.
4. Heat to boiling. Cook quickly for 20 minutes. Remove from heat and measure juice. (You should have 5 cups.)
5. Heat juice and sugar to boiling. Boil rapidly until jelly tests for set, about 15 minutes. Seal in hot sterilized glasses.

NOTE:

A chef's trick—add a tablespoon of Concord Grape Jelly to roast veal gravy. Or while cooking vension (any cut), add to the sauce. Good to serve with crackers and assorted cheese.

Guava Jelly

Cooking time: 10 minutes

Yield: 9 8-ounce glasses

2½ pounds ripe guavas

4½ cups water

2 lemons, juice of

1 box (1¾ ounces) powdered pectin

7 cups sugar

METHOD:

1. Slice guavas. Combine with water in a heavy kettle.
2. Heat to boiling. Cover. Simmer 5 minutes. Crush fruit. Place in a jelly bag, and drain.
3. Combine guava juice, lemon juice, and pectin in the same kettle. Heat to a hard boil. Stir in sugar. Bring to a *full rolling boil* (a boil that cannot be stirred down with a wooden spoon). Boil 1 minute, stirring constantly.
4. Remove from heat. Stir and skim for 5 minutes. Seal in hot sterilized glasses.

NOTE:

Guava Jelly goes perfectly with a tropical-fruit salad plate and crisp crackers.

Litchi Jam

Cooking time: 30 minutes

Yield: 4 8-ounce glasses

6 cups canned litchis

2 cups sugar

4 lemons, juice of

METHOD:

1. Drain syrup from litchis into a heavy kettle. Stir in sugar and lemon juice.
2. Heat to boiling. Simmer 10 minutes. Add litchis and simmer 10 minutes. Remove pits with a slotted spoon as they come to the surface. Cook until jam tests for set, about 10 minutes. Seal in hot sterilized glasses.

NOTE:

Originally from China, the litchi (or lichee) is a red fruit that grows in Hawaii, ripens in June and July, and is then sold in the markets in bunches. Fresh litchis, shelled and pitted, are sweet and juicy and a great addition to fresh fruit salad or cocktail. Canned litchis from the Orient are delicious in their own syrup.

Use Litchi Jam as a jam, ice-cream topping, or as the Chinese do—with a fried fish or shellfish.

Mango-Apple Jam

Cooking time: 1 hour

Yield: 9 8-ounce glasses

    5 firm mangoes, about 5 pounds
    3 large cooking apples, about 1 pound
    1 lemon, thinly sliced
    3 cups water
    5 cups sugar

METHOD:

1. Peel mangoes and slice thin. Peel, core, and slice apples. Tie apple peels and lemon slices in a piece of cheesecloth. Combine fruits, peel bag, and water in a heavy kettle.
2. Heat to boiling. Simmer until fruits are soft, about 15 minutes. Remove peel bag. Add sugar. Cook, stirring frequently, until jam thickens, about 45 minutes. Seal in hot sterilized glasses.

NOTE:

To this jam you may add ½ teaspoon allspice for that different taste.

Mango Jam

Cooking time: 1 hour

Yield: 9 8-ounce glasses

    6 firm mangoes, about 6 pounds
    4 cups water
    1 lemon, juice of
    6 cups sugar

METHOD:

1. Peel and slice mangoes. Place in a heavy kettle with water and lemon juice.
2. Heat to boiling. Cook, stirring often, until mangoes are tender, about 15 minutes. (If mixture is stringy, press through a sieve.)
3. Add sugar to kettle. Cook, stirring frequently, until jam thickens, about 45 minutes. Seal in hot sterilized glasses.

NOTE:

An oblong fruit about the size of a large pear, the mango is green in color, turning orange-yellow when ripe, and has a delicious, pleasantly acid pulp. Of East Indian origin, the mango tree is now cultivated in southern Florida and in California. Mangoes are in season from May to September. They are also available canned and as nectar.

Thin your Mango Jam with a little pineapple juice to make a delicious topping for vanilla ice cream.

Mint-Apple Jelly

Cooking time: 1 hour

Yield: 5 8-ounce glasses

    6 medium-size cooking apples,
      about 2 pounds
    4 cups water
    1 teaspoon lemon juice
    3 cups fresh mint sprigs
    4 cups sugar
      peppermint extract (optional)
      green food coloring (optional)

METHOD:

1. Core apples, and cut into quarters. Place apples, water, and lemon juice in a heavy kettle.
2. Heat to boiling. Simmer until apples are mushy, about 25 minutes. Place in a jelly bag, and drain overnight.

3. Tie mint in a piece of cheesecloth. Combine with apple juice and sugar in the same kettle. Heat to boiling. Boil until jelly tests for set, about 30 minutes.
4. Remove mint bag. Add a few drops of peppermint extract and green food coloring, if desired. Seal in hot sterilized glasses.

NOTE:

I have tried this recipe using dried mint. It was not a success. The tang and aroma and taste of the fresh mint is needed. This jelly is a wonderful accompaniment to roast lamb. I sometimes fill the centers of pear or peach halves with a spoonful of Mint-Apple Jelly, and serve with cottage cheese. Diluted, it is an unusual and tasty topping for lime, lemon, and pineapple sherbet.

Mint-Crab Apple Jelly

Cooking time: 1 hour

Yield: 3 8-ounce glasses

12 medium-size crab apples,
about 2 pounds
2 cups water
4 cups sugar
2 tablespoons vinegar
2 cups fresh mint sprigs

METHOD:

1. Chop apples. Place apples and water in a heavy kettle.
2. Heat to boiling. Simmer until apples are soft, about 30 minutes. Place in a jelly bag and drain overnight.
3. The next day, heat juice in the same kettle to boiling. Add sugar, and stir until sugar dissolves. Boil until jelly tests for set, about 30 minutes. Add vinegar and mint, stirring well. Seal in hot sterilized glasses.

NOTE:

When crab apples are in season they are found in such abundance that I hope you will make this jelly (6 medium-size cooking apples may be substituted if crab apples are unobtainable). It is delicious with lamb chops and pork chops.

Orange-Wine Jelly

Cooking time: 5 minutes

Yield: 3 8-ounce glasses

3¼ cups sugar
1¼ cups white wine
½ bottle (3 ounces) liquid pectin
1 can (6 ounces) frozen concentrated
orange juice, thawed

METHOD:

1. Combine sugar and wine in a heavy kettle.
2. Bring to a *full rolling boil*. Boil hard 1 minute.
3. Remove from heat. Stir in liquid pectin and thawed juice until well mixed. Seal in hot sterilized glasses.

NOTE:

This is a perfect way to use up the wine left over from your last dinner party. Serve with cold sliced chicken or lamb.

Papaya-Pineapple Jam

Cooking time: 40 minutes

Yield: 10 8-ounce glasses

- 3 oranges
- 4 lemons
- 1 large ripe pineapple
- 2 large papayas
- 10 cups sugar
- ¼ teaspoon oil of ginger (optional)
      or
- 1 teaspoon ground ginger

METHOD:

1. Grate the rinds of 1 orange and 1 lemon. Squeeze all oranges and lemons. Tie orange and lemon seeds in a piece of cheesecloth.
2. Slice, peel, core, and cube pineapple. Peel, seed, and cube papayas.
3. Combine juices, rinds, and seed bag in a heavy kettle. Heat to boiling. Remove seed bag. Add cubed fruits and sugar.
4. Heat to boiling, stirring frequently. Simmer until mixture thickens, about 30 minutes. Stir in oil of ginger or ground ginger. Seal in hot sterilized glasses.

NOTE:

A bright sunshine color. Goes well with French toast, waffles, and pancakes.

Peach Jam

Cooking time: about 40 minutes

Yield: 4 8-ounce glasses

- 12 large, ripe peaches, about 3 pounds
- 1 bottle (4 ounces) maraschino cherries, drained
- 4 cups sugar
- 1 orange, juice and rind

METHOD:

1. Peel, pit, and quarter peaches. Grind peaches and cherries in a food grinder, using a fine blade.

2. Place sugar-and-peach mixture in a heavy kettle with orange juice and rind. Heat to boiling.
3. Cook over low heat, stirring often, until mixture thickens, about 40 minutes. Seal in hot sterilized glasses.

NOTE:

You may add some of the cherry juice if you want to give the jam a red color. This colorful jam is marvelous to serve at an elegant dinner party with homemade butterhorn rolls.

Low Calorie Peach Jam

Cooking time: 45 minutes

Yield: 6 8-ounce glasses

- 12 ripe peaches, about 3 pounds
- ½ cup water
- 48 saccharin tablets
- 4 cups glycerine

METHOD:

1. Peel peaches. Place in a heavy kettle with water.
2. Heat to boiling. Cook, stirring several times, until fruit softens, about 40 minutes. Remove pits with slotted spoon.
3. Remove ½ cup hot liquid from kettle. Dissolve saccharin tablets in hot liquid. Stir into kettle with glycerine.
4. Cook until jam thickens, about 5 minutes. Seal in hot sterilized glasses.

NOTE:

Try this jam with plain yogurt for a slenderizing summer lunch.

Pear-Ginger Jam

Cooking time: 45 minutes

Yield: 12 8-ounce glasses

12 medium-size ripe pears, about 4 pounds
8 cups sugar
½ cup chopped preserved ginger
  or
½ cup candied ginger, chopped
2 lemons, seeded and finely chopped

METHOD:
1. Peel, core, and chop pears. Combine with sugar, ginger, and lemons in a heavy kettle. Cover. Allow to stand overnight.
2. The next day, heat to boiling, and cook quickly for 10 minutes, stirring often. Reduce heat, and cook until yellow and clear, about 35 minutes. Seal in hot sterilized glasses.

NOTE:
Nice to eat with yogurt or as ice-cream topping or filling for layer cake.

Green Pepper Jelly

Cooking time: 15 minutes

Yield: 9 8-ounce glasses

4 large sweet green peppers,
  seeded and chopped
1 small hot red pepper,
  seeded and chopped
6½ cups sugar
1½ cups cider vinegar
1 bottle (6 ounces) liquid pectin
  green food coloring

METHOD:
1. Combine peppers, sugar, and vinegar in a heavy kettle. Heat to boiling. Boil 10 minutes.
2. Remove from heat, and allow to stand for 15 minutes. Return to heat, and boil 2 minutes.
3. Strain out chopped peppers. Stir in pectin. Stir, skimming if necessary, 5 minutes. Tint a pale green with several drops of green food coloring. Seal in hot sterilized glasses.

NOTE:
An unusual jelly to star at a picnic or barbecue with grilled franks and hamburgers.

Green and Red Pepper Jelly

Cooking time: 15.minutes

Yield: 4 8-ounce glasses

1 cup sugar
1½ cups cider vinegar
3 large sweet green peppers,
  seeded and chopped
3 large sweet red peppers,
  seeded and chopped
½ bottle (3 ounces) liquid pectin

METHOD:
1. Combine sugar and vinegar in a heavy kettle. Heat to a rolling boil.
2. Add chopped pepper. Boil 15 minutes. Remove from heat. Stir in pectin. Stir, skimming if necessary, 5 minutes. Allow to stand 2 hours. Seal in hot sterilized glasses.

NOTE:
Sweet peppers are green when mature, but turn red after that and are found in food stores in both stages of development.

Try Green and Red Pepper Jelly at a smorgasbord supper or barbecue.

Pineapple-Apricot Jam

Cooking time: 12 minutes

Yield: 8 8-ounce glasses

- **1 can (1 pound 13 ounces) pineapple tidbits, drained**
- **1 can (1 pound 13 ounces) apricot halves, drained and cut up**
- **5½ cups sugar**
- **1 large lemon, juice of**
- **1 bottle (6 ounces) liquid pectin**

METHOD:

1. Combine the drained fruits, sugar, and lemon juice in a heavy kettle. Stir over low heat until sugar dissolves.
2. Bring mixture to a full rolling boil, boil rapidly for 2 minutes.
3. Remove from heat, stir in pectin. Stir for 5 minutes to keep fruit well distributed. Skim.
4. Seal in hot sterilized glasses.

NOTE:

A nice addition to a table spread for afternoon tea. Also delicious with plain yogurt for a quick lunch.

Pineapple-Mint Jelly

Cooking time: 15 minutes

Yield: 3 8-ounce glasses

- **2 cups canned sweetened pineapple juice**
- **1½ cups sugar**
- **3 lemons, juice of**
- **1 tablespoon chopped fresh mint**

METHOD:

1. Place pineapple juice in a heavy saucepan.
2. Heat to boiling. Add sugar and lemon juice, and stir until sugar dissolves.
3. Boil rapidly until jelly tests for set, about 15 minutes. Stir in chopped mint. Seal in hot sterilized glasses.

NOTE:

Nice with chicken salad.

Pineapple-Strawberry Jam

Cooking time: 15 minutes

Yield: 8 8-ounce glasses

- **1 package (10 ounces) frozen sliced strawberries**
- **1 can (1 pound 4 ounces) crushed pineapple**
- **1 lemon, juice and rind**
- **3 oranges, juice and rind**
- **4½ cups sugar**
- **½ bottle (3 ounces) liquid pectin**

METHOD:

1. Combine fruits, citrus juice, and rind.
2. Stir in sugar, and cook over medium heat until sugar is completely dissolved.
3. Bring to a full rolling boil. Boil rapidly for 1 minute.
4. Stir in pectin, and remove from heat.
5. Stir for about 5 minutes to keep fruit distributed. Skim.
6. Seal in hot sterilized glasses.

NOTE:

Pineapple-Strawberry Jam has a beautiful color and a very aromatic flavor. Serve it in a crystal dish to be spooned onto toast fingers spread with cream cheese.

Easy but delicious desserts can be assembled from a well-stocked cupboard of jams and jellies. Combinations pictured here are: Mint-Apple Jelly with lemon sherbet, Apple-Pineapple Jam with plain yogurt, Raspberry Jam with cheesecake, and Blueberry Jam with vanilla ice cream.

Plum-Raspberry Jam

Cooking time: 30 minutes

Yield: 8 8-ounce glasses

- **4 pounds blue or red plums**
- **2 packages (10½ ounces each) frozen red raspberries, thawed**
- **6 cups sugar**

METHOD:

1. Remove pits from plums. Grind plums in a food grinder, using a fine blade.
2. Mix plums with raspberries and stir in sugar.
3. Cook over medium heat, stirring often, until mixture thickens, about 30 minutes.
4. Seal in hot sterilized glasses.

NOTE:

Blue and red plums are about the size of a peach, with gold-colored flesh that yields to the touch when ripe. If you use blue plums when making this recipe, the jam comes out a lovely deep maroon; if red plums are used, the jam is a deep red.

Beach Plum Jam

Cooking time: 40 minutes

Yield: 8 8-ounce glasses

- **6 cups stemmed beach plums, about 3 pounds**
- **4 cups water**
- **6 cups sugar**

METHOD:

1. Cover beach plums with water in a heavy kettle. Heat to boiling. Drain. Return beach plums to kettle. Add 4 cups water.

2. Heat to boiling. Simmer 15 minutes, mashing with a wooden spoon to extract juice. Press mixture through a sieve to remove pits.
3. Return fruit to kettle. Heat to boiling. Add sugar and stir until sugar dissolves. Cook, stirring and skimming several times, until jam tests for set, about 20 minutes. Seal in hot sterilized glasses.

NOTE:

This fruit was a joy to the early settlers along the Atlantic. You have to gather beach plums yourself in coastal areas. When ripe, their thick, tough skin is much like that of a wild purple grape, with the firmness and bitter flavor not unlike a wild cherry.

Beach Plum Jelly

Cooking time: 20 minutes

Yield: 8 8-ounce glasses

- **6 cups beach plums, stemmed, about 3 pounds**
- **½ cup water**
- **6½ cups sugar**
- **2 tablespoons lemon juice**
- **1 bottle (6 ounces) liquid pectin**

METHOD:

1. Place beach plums and water in a heavy kettle. Mash with a wooden spoon to extract juice.
2. Heat to boiling. Cover kettle. Simmer 15 minutes. Place in a jelly bag, and drain overnight.
3. Combine fruit juice, sugar, and lemon juice in same kettle. Bring to a full rolling boil, cook 1 minute stirring constantly.
4. Remove from heat, and stir in pectin. Stir 5 minutes. Skim. Seal in hot sterilized glasses.

NOTE:

A marvelous breakfast jelly with just enough tartness to make it a year-around favorite with toast and English muffins.

Low Calorie Damson Plum Jam

Cooking time: 25 minutes

Yield: 5 8-ounce glasses

- 18 Damson plums, about 3 pounds
- ½ cup water
- 48 saccharin tablets
- 4 cups glycerine

METHOD:
1. Place fruit and water in a heavy kettle.
2. Heat to boiling. Cook, stirring several times, until fruit softens, about 20 minutes. Remove plum pits with slotted spoon.
3. Remove ½ cup hot liquid from kettle. Dissolve saccharin tablets in hot liquid. Stir into kettle with glycerine.
4. Cook until jam thickens, about 5 minutes. Seal in hot sterilized glasses.

NOTE:
Damson plums are very small and firm and either purple or yellow in color. If you are watching your weight, try this jam with yogurt or cottage cheese.

Greengage Plum Jam

Cooking time: 25 minutes

Yield: 6 8-ounce glasses

- 12 slightly underripe greengage plums, about 2 pounds
- 1 cup water
- 4 cups sugar

METHOD:
1. Halve and pit plums. Tie pits in a piece of cheesecloth. Combine plums, bag with pits, and water in a heavy kettle.
2. Heat to boiling. Simmer until fruit is tender, about 15 minutes. Add sugar and stir until sugar dissolves.
3. Heat to a rolling boil. Cook, skimming as necessary, until jam tests for set, about 10 minutes.

4. Allow to cool, then stir to distribute fruit. Remove pit bag. Seal in hot sterilized glasses.

NOTE:
Greengage plums are small, round, and greenish-yellow in color. Hot biscuits and whole-wheat toast taste special with this jam.

Pomegranate Jam

Cooking time: 45 minutes

Yield: 4 8-ounce glasses

- 4 firm pomegranates
- 1 cup water
- 4 cups sugar

METHOD:
1. Halve pomegranates and place in a heavy kettle with water.
2. Heat to boiling. Cook, stirring often, until pomegranates are mushy, about 30 minutes, being careful that fruit does not burn.
3. Press mixture through a sieve to remove seeds. Return pulp to kettle and add sugar. Stir until sugar dissolves.
4. Heat mixture to boiling. Cook, stirring often, until jam tests for set, about 15 minutes. Seal in hot sterilized glasses.

NOTE:
This is a jam you can make around Christmas time when pomegranates are available. Wrap in your prettiest papers and give glasses of Pomegranate Jam to good friends for Christmas.

Pomegranate Jelly

Cooking time: 15–20 minutes

Yield: 6 8-ounce glasses

4 firm pomegranates, about 4 pounds
4 cups sugar

METHOD:

1. Halve pomegranates, and place in a large baking dish. Cover dish.
2. Bake in a very slow oven, 250 degrees, 2 hours, or until fruits are pulpy and the juice flows freely. Place in a jelly bag and drain overnight.
3. The next day, heat juice to boiling in a heavy kettle. Add sugar, and stir until sugar dissolves. Boil until jelly tests for set, about 15 minutes. Seal in hot sterilized glasses.

NOTE:

A refreshing jelly. Serve with corn bread or coffee cake for breakfast.

Quince Jam

Cooking time: 35 minutes

Yield: 3 8-ounce glasses

6 ripe quinces, about 1 pound
1½ cups water
2 cups sugar
½ lemon, juice of

METHOD:

1. Peel, core, and cut up quinces, or grate quinces. Combine with water in a heavy kettle.
2. Heat to boiling. Simmer until quinces are soft, about 15 minutes. Add sugar, and stir until sugar dissolves. Add lemon juice.
3. Boil rapidly, stirring often, until jam tests for set, about 20 minutes. Seal in hot sterilized glasses.

NOTE:

Lucky the family that has a quince tree in the garden!

The round or pear-shaped fruit of the tree is full of natural pectin and is used for making jams, jellies, marmalades, butters, or cheeses, and syrups. It is necessary to cook quinces before they can be eaten. Quince trees are usually found in areas of this country where apples grow; they are planted mostly as flowering trees, and the fruit is a bonus.

Quince Jelly

Cooking time: 2 hours 40 minutes

Yield: 5 8-ounce glasses

6 quinces, about 1 pound
water
5 cups sugar

METHOD:

1. Peel, and core quinces. Place in a heavy kettle with enough water to float the fruit.
2. Heat to boiling. Simmer until quinces are tender, about 2 hours 30 minutes. Place in a jelly bag, and drain overnight.
3. The next day, heat juice to boiling in the same kettle. Add sugar, and stir until sugar dissolves. Boil until jelly tests for set, about 10 minutes.
4. Remove from heat, and allow to cool. Seal in hot sterilized glasses.

NOTE:

The tart flavor of Quince Jelly makes it a special breakfast treat.

Quince-Apple Jam

Cooking time: 35 minutes

Yield: 6 8-ounce glasses

6 ripe quinces, about 1 pound
3 large cooking apples, about 1 pound
¼ cup water
4 cups sugar
1 lemon, juice of

METHOD:

1. Peel, core, and cut up quinces and apples (or grate fruit). Combine with water in a heavy kettle.
2. Heat to boiling. Simmer until quinces are soft, about 15 minutes. Add sugar and stir until sugar dissolves. Add lemon juice.
3. Boil rapidly, stirring often, until jam tests for set, about 20 minutes. Seal in hot sterilized glasses.

NOTE:

Quince jams are rather tart. Nice for breakfast with French toast, topped with powdered sugar.

Raspberry Jam

Cooking time: 35 minutes.

Yield: 4 8-ounce glasses

8 cups fresh red raspberries, about 2 pounds
5 cups sugar

METHOD:

1. Place raspberries in a heavy kettle. Heat to boiling. Simmer 3 minutes.
2. Add sugar and stir until sugar dissolves. Heat to boiling. Simmer, skimming if necessary, until jam tests for set, about 30 minutes. Seal in hot sterilized glasses.

NOTE:

Raspberry Jam makes a lovely topping for a chilled cheesecake, not to mention its popularity at breakfast and at lunch with peanut butter sandwiches.

Seedless Raspberry Jam

Cooking time: 50 minutes

Yield: 10 8-ounce glasses

16 cups fresh red raspberries, about 4 pounds
2 cups red currant juice
12 cups sugar

METHOD:

1. Combine raspberries and currant juice in a heavy kettle.
2. Heat to boiling. Cook, mashing fruit with a wooden spoon, until soft, about 30 minutes. Press mixture through a fine sieve to remove seeds.
3. Combine raspberry juice and sugar in the same kettle. Heat to boiling. Cook until jam tests for set, about 20 minutes. Allow to cool. Seal in hot sterilized glasses.

NOTE:

Try a bit of Seedless Raspberry Jam with vanilla ice cream or tapioca pudding.

Low Calorie Raspberry Jam

Cooking time: 20 minutes

Yield: 5 8-ounce glasses

12 cups red raspberries, about 3 pounds
¼ cup water
48 saccharin tablets
4 cups glycerine

METHOD:
1. Place raspberries with water in a heavy kettle.
2. Heat to boiling. Cook, stirring several times, until juice runs, about 15 minutes.
3. Remove ½ cup hot juice from kettle. Dissolve saccharin tablets in hot juice. Stir into kettle with glycerine.
4. Cook until jam thickens, about 5 minutes. Seal in hot sterilized glasses.

NOTE:
Serve with cottage cheese or plain yogurt for a touch of sweetness in a low-calorie diet.

Oven Raspberry Jam

Cooking time: 15 minutes

Yield: 12 8-ounce glasses

16 cups fresh red raspberries, about 4 pounds
10 cups sugar

METHOD:
1. Wash and dry raspberries on paper towels. Place in a large baking dish and cover. Place sugar in a second large baking dish.
2. Bake sugar and raspberries in a very slow oven (250 degrees) for 15 minutes or until fruit is hot but not boiling.

3. Beat raspberries to a mush with a wooden spoon. Gradually add the hot sugar until sugar dissolves. Seal in hot sterilized glasses.

NOTE:
Serve with poached fresh pears and a swirl of whipped cream.

Raspberry-Rhubarb Jam

Cooking time: 45 minutes

Yield: 7 8-ounce glasses

9 cups cut-up rhubarb, about 3 pounds
2 oranges, juice and rind
4 cups red raspberries, about 1 pound
5 cups sugar

METHOD:
1. Combine rhubarb and orange juice and rind in a heavy kettle.
2. Heat to boiling, slowly. Add raspberries and sugar, and stir until sugar dissolves.
3. Cook, stirring and skimming several times, until jam tests for set, about 30 minutes. Seal in hot sterilized glasses.

NOTE:
For memorable eating, serve this bright red jam on thick slices of sourdough bread.

Rhubarb-Blueberry Jam

Cooking time: about 10 minutes

Yield: 7 8-ounce glasses

    1½ pounds rhubarb, about 6 cups, cut up
    ½   cup water
    6   cups blueberries, crushed, 3 pints
    7   cups sugar
    1   bottle (6 ounces) liquid pectin

METHOD:

1. Chop rhubarb, add water, and cook over low heat until soft.
2. Add the blueberries and sugar, mix well, Cook over low heat a few minutes until sugar is completely dissolved.
3. Bring to a full rolling boil, and boil rapidly for 1 minute, stirring constantly.
4. Stir in pectin, and immediately remove from heat.
5. Stir for 5 minutes to keep fruit well distributed. Skim.
6. Seal in hot sterilized glasses.

NOTE:

An unusual, but very good, combination of flavors. Split hot biscuits, fill with Rhubarb-Blueberry Jam, and top with whipped cream for a delicious quick cobbler.

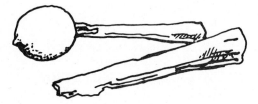

Rhubarb-Mixed Peel Jam

Cooking time: 45 minutes

Yield: 10 8-ounce glasses

    12 cups cut-up rhubarb, about 4 pounds
     4 large oranges, peel of—thinly sliced
     4 large lemons, peel of—thinly sliced
     8 cups sugar

METHOD:

1. Layer rhubarb, orange and lemon peels, and sugar in a large kettle. Cover kettle, and allow to stand overnight.
2. The next day, strain the juice from the fruit mixture, and pour into a heavy kettle.
3. Heat to boiling. Boil syrup for 15 minutes. Pour over fruits in kettle. Cover, and allow to stand overnight.
4. The next day, boil the fruit mixture until jam tests for set, about 30 minutes. Seal in hot sterilized glasses.

NOTE:

Many people who do not like rhubarb will nevertheless appreciate this recipe.

Strawberry Jam, Number I

Cooking time: 20 minutes

Yield: 6 8-ounce glasses

    8   cups firm strawberries, 2 quarts
    3½ cups sugar
    2   lemons, juice of
            or
    2   cups red currant juice

METHOD:

1. Wash, hull, and dry strawberries on paper towels.
2. Combine berries and sugar in a heavy kettle. Heat very slowly until sugar dissolves. Add lemon or red currant juice.
3. Boil steadily until jam tests for set, about 12 minutes. Cool and stir to distribute fruit. Seal in hot sterilized glasses.

NOTE:

Serve Strawberry Jam with pancakes, waffles, biscuits, muffins, ice cream, peanut butter, and much more. This is a versatile, popular jam.

Strawberry Jam, Number II

Cooking time: 20 minutes

Yield: 4 8-ounce glasses

    4 cups firm strawberries, 1 quart
    2 cups sugar
    1 lemon, juice of

METHOD:
1. Wash, hull, and dry strawberries on paper towels.
2. Combine sugar and lemon juice in a heavy kettle. Stir until sugar dissolves.
3. Heat to boiling, stirring constantly, until mixture forms a syrup. Add strawberries. Remove kettle from heat. Allow strawberries to stand in syrup for 15 minutes.
4. Return kettle to heat, and boil until jam tests for set, about 5 minutes. Cool, and stir to distribute fruit. Seal in hot sterilized glasses.

NOTE:
Try unsweetened whipped cream and this Strawberry Jam with your best homemade biscuits for a delicious shortcake when fresh strawberries aren't in season.

Low Calorie Strawberry Jam

Cooking time: 20 minutes

Yield: 5 8-ounce glasses

    12 cups ripe strawberries, about 3 quarts
    ¼ cup water
    48 saccharin tablets
    4 cups glycerine

METHOD:
1. Hull strawberries. Place strawberries with water in a heavy kettle.
2. Heat to boiling. Cook, stirring several times, until juice runs, about 15 minutes.
3. Remove ½ cup hot juice from kettle. Dissolve saccharin tablets in hot juice. Stir into kettle with glycerine.
4. Cook until jam thickens, about 5 minutes. Seal in hot sterilized glasses.

NOTE:
If you are trying to cut down on sugar in your diet, low-calorie jams are the answer. Also, if you have a friend who is a diabetic, Low Calorie Strawberry Jam makes a much-appreciated gift.

Strawberry-Gooseberry Jelly

Cooking time: 15 minutes

Yield: 4 8-ounce glasses

    4 cups ripe strawberries, 1 quart
    3 cups gooseberries (red if possible),
      1 pound
    ½ cup water
    4 cups sugar
    2 lemons, juice of

METHOD:
1. Hull strawberries. Combine with gooseberries and water in a heavy kettle.
2. Heat to boiling. Cook, mashing the berries to extract juice, until soft, about 10 minutes. Place in a jelly bag, and drain overnight.
3. The next day, combine fruit juice, sugar, and lemon juice in a kettle. Heat to boiling. Boil until jelly tests for set, about 5 minutes. Seal in hot sterilized glasses.

NOTE:
This jelly makes really good eating with hot biscuits. Nice in omelets too.

Strawberry-Pineapple Jam

Cooking time: 35 minutes

Yield: 7 8-ounce glasses

8 cups firm strawberries, 2 quarts
1 can (8 ounces) crushed pineapple
1 lemon, juice and rind
4 cups sugar

METHOD:

1. Wash, hull, and drain strawberries on paper towels. Combine berries, pineapple, lemon juice, and rind in a heavy kettle.
2. Heat slowly, stirring gently, until juice flows from berries. Add sugar, and stir until sugar dissolves. Heat to boiling, and simmer until thickened, about 20 minutes. Seal in hot sterilized glasses.

NOTE:

Strawberry-Pineapple Jam makes a delicious topping for cream pies.

Green Tomato Jam

Cooking time: 40 minutes

Yield: 10 8-ounce glasses

16 green tomatoes, about 4 pounds
6 cups sugar
few cloves
1 lemon, rind of

METHOD:

1. Peel tomatoes by plunging into boiling water until skins burst. Core and cut into wedges. Combine with sugar, cloves, and chopped lemon rind in a heavy kettle.
2. Heat to boiling. Boil briskly, stirring and skimming often, until jam tests for set, about 20 minutes. Seal in hot sterilized glasses.

NOTE:

This is the perfect spread for hamburgers cooked over a charcoal fire.

Tomato-Pineapple Jam

Cooking time: 45 minutes

Yield: 8 8-ounce glasses

16 green tomatoes, about 4 pounds
5 cups sugar
1 can (8 ounces) crushed pineapple
1 lemon, juice of

METHOD:

1. Peel tomatoes by plunging into boiling water until skins burst. Core and cut into thin slices. Combine with sugar in a heavy kettle.
2. Heat to boiling. Cook, stirring often, until tomatoes are soft, about 20 minutes. Stir in crushed pineapple, and boil for 15 minutes. Add lemon juice, and boil and skim until jam tests for set, about 10 minutes. Seal in hot sterilized glasses.

NOTE:

This jam goes particularly well with sliced cold meat loaf.

Red Tomato Jam

Cooking time: 1 hour

Yield: 5 8-ounce glasses

  9 ripe tomatoes, about 3 pounds
4½ pounds sugar
  2 lemons, juice of
  1 teaspoon ground ginger

METHOD:
1. Peel tomatoes by plunging into boiling water until the skins burst. Core and cut into slices. Combine sliced tomatoes, sugar, lemon juice, and ground ginger in a heavy kettle.
2. Heat to boiling. Cook, stirring and skimming, until mixture thickens, about 1 hour. Cool and stir to distribute fruit. Seal in hot sterilized glasses.

NOTE:
Tomato jams are nice to use in omelets or as accompaniments to fish or cheese dishes.

Vinegar-Mint Jelly

Cooking time: 10 minutes

Yield: 2 8-ounce glasses

  1 cup sugar
  1 cup water
  1 envelope unflavored gelatin
 ½ cup white vinegar
  3 tablespoons chopped fresh mint
     green food coloring

METHOD:
1. Combine sugar and water in a heavy saucepan.
2. Heat to boiling. Simmer to make a syrup, about 5 minutes. Soften gelatin in vinegar. Stir into boiling syrup until gelatin dissolves.
3. Add mint and a few drops of green food coloring, and simmer several minutes. Seal in hot sterilized glasses. Store in refrigerator.

NOTE:
This jelly goes perfectly with roast pork or veal steaks.

Marmalades and Conserves

Marmalades are soft fruit jellies containing small pieces of fruit or peel evenly suspended throughout the mixture. They should be cooked in relatively small batches, and after the sugar is added, cooked rapidly to, or almost to, the setting point. A spoonful of marmalade added to corn-muffin batter, coffee-cake ingredients, or a pound-cake mixture imparts a wonderful flavor.

Conserves are jamlike products that differ from jams in possessing more density and chewiness. A true conserve usually contains nuts, raisins, or other dried fruits.

Conserves should also be made in small batches. Cook rapidly after the sugar has dissolved, and add nuts, if desired, near the end of the cooking time. Both conserves and marmalades provide unusual toppings for ice cream, puddings, pancakes, and waffles.

You will be surprised to see that some of my marmalade recipes call for salt. This little flavor trick probably originated back in the days of sailing ships. Oranges grown in Spain were sliced and packed in wooden kegs. Once the ships had cleared the harbor, the kegs were opened, filled with fresh seawater, then sealed for their voyage to the marmalade factories in Scotland. The salt water preserved the oranges on their long journey.

Anyone who has tasted real Scotch marmalade knows how delicious it is. So try a little salt when making your marmalade.

Hints for Making Marmalades and Conserves

Generally speaking, the same directions for making jams and jellies apply to marmalades and conserves. Here are some further suggestions.

1. Peel from oranges, lemons, and grapefruit may be cut by hand or put through an electric or hand chopper. If prepared by hand, you can have thinner or thicker pieces of peel. The choice is yours.

2. The more white pith you retain on the shredded peel, the more bitter the marmalade will be. You should keep part of the pith or the seeds, for both have a high degree of setting quality. Tie some pith and seeds in a piece of cheesecloth and cook along with the juice, sugar, and shredded peels.

3. Consider warming your sugar before adding it.

4. If sugar is added before the peel is tender, the peel will tend to toughen, and this will spoil your marmalade. To test for tenderness, take a little peel in your fingers, and rub it almost to nothing. If you cannot do this, continue cooking until you can.

5. Although citrus fruits do set well, this setting property can be lost by overcooking. Test often during cooking for set or jell.

6. When marmalade has reached the setting point, remove the pan from the heat. Allow it to cool a little, stir well to distribute the peel and fruit, then add, if you like, a sprinkle of salt. Cooling the marmalade provides a firmer product, and prevents peel and fruit from sinking to bottom of glass.

7. Seal with paraffin in sterilized glasses or jars.

Apple-Orange Peel Marmalade

Cooking time: 1 hour

Yield: 8 8-ounce glasses

- 1 pound orange peel (10 medium oranges)
- 6 cups water
- 3 tart cooking apples, peeled, cored, and quartered, about 1 pound
- 6 cups sugar
- pinch of ground ginger (optional)

METHOD:
1. Use a sharp paring knife to peel oranges. Shred or cut peel in thin or thick strips as desired.
2. Soak peel overnight in water. The next day, simmer the peel until almost soft, about 30 minutes.
3. Add the apples, and continue cooking until soft, about 20 minutes. Stir frequently to prevent scorching.
4. Add sugar and ginger, and stir until dissolved. Cook rapidly for 10 minutes, then test for set. Remove from heat.
5. Allow to cool for about 30 minutes. Stir well to distribute peel. Seal in hot sterilized glasses.

NOTE:
Chill and serve as an accompaniment to baked ham.

Banana Marmalade

Cooking time: 30 minutes

Yield: 4 8-ounce glasses

- 6 medium-size ripe bananas, about 2 pounds
- 3 cups sugar
- 2 lemons, juice and grated rind

METHOD:
1. Peel firm yellow bananas, slice into half-inch rounds. Discard blemished or too-soft sections.
2. Combine all ingredients in top of double boiler, and stir over hot water until sugar dissolves.
3. Place top of double boiler over direct heat. Cook, and stir over low heat until mixture is thick and smooth, about 15 minutes.
4. Bring to a rapid boil, and cook quickly until mixture thickens and sets. Stir continuously at this stage, or mixture will stick and burn.
5. Seal in hot sterilized glasses, cool, and refrigerate. This marmalade will keep in the refrigerator for about 6 weeks.

NOTE:
Try my very special banana shortcake. Split store-bought sponge layers, fill and top with sliced ripe bananas. Spread each layer of bananas with Banana Marmalade, and top with whipped cream. Forget the calories, and enjoy.

Carrot Marmalade

Cooking time: 10 minutes

Yield: 6 8-ounce glasses

- 8 large carrots, about 2 pounds
- 2 oranges, seeded and cut up
- 1 cup fresh or bottled lemon juice
- 7 cups sugar
- 1 bottle (6 ounces) liquid pectin

METHOD:
1. Put carrots and oranges in blender. Process until finely chopped.
2. Combine with lemon juice and sugar.
3. Cook slowly for a few minutes until sugar dissolves. Bring to a full rolling boil. Boil rapidly for 1 minute stirring constantly.
4. Remove from heat, and stir in pectin. Stir 5 minutes to distribute solids. Skim.
5. Seal in hot sterilized glasses.

NOTE:
This colorful, tangy marmalade makes a great glaze for baked ham.

Red Cherry Conserve

Cooking time: 40 minutes

Yield: 8 8-ounce glasses

- 10 cups sour red cherries, about 2½ pounds
- 1 cup raisins
- 6 cups sugar
- 1 lemon, juice of
    or
- ¼ teaspoon citric acid
- 2 cups chopped walnuts

METHOD:

1. Stem and pit cherries. Tie pits in a piece of cheesecloth. Place cherries, raisins and cheesecloth in a heavy kettle.
2. Heat slowly, stirring often, until cherries are soft, about 20 minutes. Add sugar and lemon juice, stirring until sugar dissolves.
3. Boil rapidly until jam tests for set, about 20 minutes. Add walnuts. Remove bag with pits.
4. Seal in hot sterilized glasses.

NOTE:

This makes a nice filling for sponge cakes and pound cakes. Spoon over vanilla ice cream for an extra rich and colorful sundae.

Date-Banana Conserve

Cooking time: 40 minutes

Yield: 6 8-ounce glasses

- 2 cups fresh dates, 1 pound
- 4 large ripe bananas, about 2 pounds
- 2 cups sugar
- 1 lemon, juice and rind

METHOD:

1. Cut dates lengthwise, and remove pits. Peel and thinly slice bananas.
2. Combine fruits, sugar, and lemon juice and rind in a heavy kettle.
3. Heat slowly to boiling. Simmer, stirring and skimming often, until jam thickens and tests for set, about 40 minutes. Seal in hot sterilized glasses.

NOTE:

Good for lunch-box sandwiches on brown bread with butter or cream cheese.

Fruit Salad Conserve

Cooking time: 40 minutes

Yield: 16 8-ounce glasses

- 1 can (1 pound) crushed pineapple
- 2 lemons, juice of
- 24 fresh apricots, 2 pounds
- 8 medium-size peaches, 2 pounds
- 10 ripe bananas
- 10 cups sugar

METHOD:

1. Drain pineapple syrup into a heavy kettle. Add lemon juice.
2. Peel, halve, pit, and slice apricots and peaches. Peel and thinly slice bananas. Add prepared fruits to kettle with crushed pineapple.
3. Heat slowly, stirring often, to boiling. Cook, stirring and skimming, until fruits are soft, about 20 minutes.
4. Add sugar, and stir until sugar dissolves. Continue cooking and stirring until fruits are clear, about 20 minutes. Seal in hot sterilized glasses.

NOTE:

This is a good seller for fund-raising projects. You may want to halve recipe for home use.

Ginger Marmalade

Cooking time: 35 minutes

Yield: 5 8-ounce glasses

> 12 tart cooking apples, about 3 pounds
> 2 cups water
>   sugar
> ½ pound preserved ginger, chopped,
>   or candied ginger

METHOD:

1. Wash apples, remove stems and blossom ends. Chop coarsely.
2. Put apples and water in a heavy kettle. Cook until apples are soft, about 25 minutes. Stir, and mash with a wooden spoon while cooking.
3. Pour into a jelly bag and let hang overnight.
4. Measure juice, and add an equal amount of sugar, cup for cup.
5. Add chopped ginger, and boil briskly for 8–10 minutes. Test for jell.
6. Let stand about 30 minutes. Stir to distribute ginger. Seal in hot sterilized glasses.

NOTE:

Excellent on hot toast, but try this marmalade with a ham sandwich for sheer perfection.

Harlequin Conserve

Cooking time: 2 hours 30 minutes

Yield: 24 8-ounce glasses

> 25 medium-size ripe peaches,
>   about 6 pounds
> 10 ripe red plums, about 1½ pounds
> 1 fresh ripe pineapple
> 1 large orange
> 2 cups seedless green grapes,
>   stemmed, 1 pound
>   sugar
> 2 cups almonds, slivered and blanched

METHOD:

1. Peel peaches. Pit peaches and plums. Tie pits in a piece of cheesecloth. Slice, peel, core, and dice pineapple. Cut whole orange into very thin slices. Combine prepared fruits, grapes, and bag with pits in a heavy kettle.
2. Heat slowly, stirring often, until fruits are soft, about 30 minutes. Measure fruits, and discard pit bag.
3. Return fruits to kettle, and add ¾ cup of sugar for every 2 cups of cooked fruit.
4. Cook very slowly, stirring often, for 20 minutes, then add almonds. Continue cooking until preserves are thick and clear, about 1 hour 30 minutes. Seal in hot sterilized glasses.

NOTE:

To prevent scorching use an asbestos pad over the gas or electric range when cooking this preserve. Colorful Harlequin Conserve makes a marvelous housewarming or Christmas gift—also a surefire winner for fund-raising occasions.

Lemon Marmalade

Cooking time: 1 hour 30 minutes

Yield: 5 8-ounce glasses

> 5 medium-size lemons, about 1 pound
> 5 cups water
> 5 cups sugar

METHOD:

1. Remove peel in thin strips, cut in slivers.
2. Pull off white pith, remove seeds, and tie in a piece of cheesecloth.
3. Combine peel, cheesecloth bag, fruit pulp, and water. Let stand overnight.

4. The next day, bring to a boil, and simmer for 1 hour. Remove bag, letting it drain well into liquid before discarding.
5. Add sugar, and stir over low heat until dissolved. Bring to a boil. Test for set after 10–15 minutes.
6. Cool for 30 minutes, stirring to distribute peel. Seal in hot sterilized glasses.

NOTE:

If desired, stir in 2 tablespoons chopped fresh mint leaves while cooking for an unusual and refreshing variation.

Lemon Marmalade is the best of all flavors on hot buttered breads.

Lemon Jelly Marmalade

Cooking time: 1 hour 15 minutes
Yield: 7 8-ounce glasses

    6 large lemons, about 1½ pounds
    7 cups water
    7 cups sugar

METHOD:

1. Remove peel in thin strips, cut in slivers, and tie in a piece of cheesecloth.
2. Pull off white pith, remove seeds, and tie in a piece of cheesecloth.
3. Combine cheesecloth bags, fruit pulp, and water. Let stand overnight.
4. The next day, bring to a boil, and simmer for 1 hour. Remove bags, letting them drain well into liquid before discarding.
5. Add sugar, and stir over low heat until dissolved. Bring to a boil. Test for set after 10–15 minutes.
6. Cool for 30 minutes. Seal in hot sterilized glasses.

NOTE:

There is no peel in this marmalade to bother those who dislike it. Good on toast with cream cheese.

Lime Marmalade

Cooking time: 1 hour 45 minutes
Yield: 5 8-ounce glasses

    8 medium-size limes, about 1 pound
    5 cups water
    5 cups sugar

METHOD:

1. Quarter limes, remove seeds, and tie in a piece of cheesecloth.
2. Finely chop limes, or process in blender.
3. Combine seeds, lime pulp and peel, and water. Let stand overnight.
4. The next day, bring to a boil, reduce heat, and cover. Simmer for about 1 hour 30 minutes, or until peel is soft, stirring frequently.
5. Remove bag of seeds, letting it drain well into liquid.
6. Stir in sugar, simmer until dissolved.
7. Bring to a boil, cook rapidly for about 10 minutes. Begin testing for set at this time. It may be necessary to cook a few more minutes.
8. Cool, stir well. Seal in hot sterilized glasses.

NOTE:

Lime Marmalade offers a tart and refreshing taste with any hot bread. I sometimes stir it, plus whipped cream, into mayonnaise for a fruit-salad dressing—delicious!

Orange Jelly Marmalade

Cooking time: 1 hour 15 minutes

Yield: 6 8-ounce glasses

3 large oranges, about 1 pound
5 cups water
5 cups sugar

METHOD:

1. Remove peel in thin strips, cut in slivers, and tie in a piece of cheesecloth.
2. Pull off white pith, and remove seeds, tie in a piece of cheesecloth.
3. Combine cheesecloth bags, fruit pulp, and water in a heavy kettle. Let stand overnight.
4. The next day, bring to a boil, and simmer for 1 hour. Remove bags, letting them drain well into liquid before discarding.
5. Add sugar, and stir over low heat until dissolved. Bring to boil. Test for set after 10–15 minutes.
6. Cool for 30 minutes. Seal in hot sterilized glasses.

NOTE:

Has the taste of marmalade without the peel. Try on warm bran muffins for a special flavor.

Bitter Orange Marmalade

Cooking time: 2 hours

Yield: 5 8-ounce glasses

3 medium Florida thin-skinned oranges, about 1 pound
4 cups water
4 cups sugar

METHOD:

1. Put the whole oranges into a heavy kettle, add water, and simmer for about 1 hour 30 minutes, or until a wooden skewer will easily pierce skin.
2. Remove oranges from liquid. Cool until they can be easily handled.
3. Halve oranges, then use a very sharp knife, or scissors, to cut into neat strips or pieces.
4. Reserve the seeds and add to liquid. Boil 10 minutes, then skim out seeds with a slotted spoon.
5. Return the cut-up oranges to liquid. Bring to a boil. Stir in sugar until it dissolves.
6. Again bring to a boil and cook rapidly, without stirring, for 10 minutes. Test for set. Continue cooking an additional 5–10 minutes until set is rechecked. Stir in a dash of salt, if desired.
7. Remove from heat, stir well and cool.
8. When cooled, stir thoroughly to distribute peel. Seal in hot sterilized glasses.

NOTE:

This is a coarse-cut, bitter marmalade—a real he-man type. Serve it with hot scones, beaten biscuits, and homemade bread.

Breakfast is a meal to look forward to and remember when you serve homemade Strawberry Jam, Apricot Jam, and Orange Marmalade with hot breads and hot coffee.

Orange-Lemon Jelly Marmalade

Cooking time: 1 hour 30 minutes

Yield: 10 8-ounce glasses

- 5 oranges, about 1½ pounds
- 7 lemons, about 1½ pounds
- 7 cups water
- 7 cups sugar

METHOD:
1. Remove peels in thin strips, cut into slivers, and tie in a piece of cheesecloth.
2. Pull off white pith and remove seeds, tie in a piece of cheesecloth.
3. Combine cheesecloth bags, fruit pulp, and water in a heavy kettle. Let stand overnight.
4. The next day, bring to a boil, and simmer for 1 hour. Remove bags, letting them drain well into liquid before discarding.
5. Add sugar, and stir over low heat until dissolved. Bring to a boil. Test for set after 30 minutes.
6. Cool for 30 minutes. Seal in hot sterilized glasses.

NOTE:
This marmalade makes an excellent glaze for Rock Cornish game hens or as a topping on warm gingerbread.

Low-Calorie Orange-Lemon Marmalade

Cooking time: 35 minutes

Yield: 3 8-ounce glasses

- 2 large juice oranges
- 2 large lemons
- 2 cups water
- 3 envelopes unflavored gelatin
- 8 saccharin tablets

METHOD:
1. Quarter and seed oranges and lemons. Cut into very thin slices. Combine with 1½ cups water in a heavy kettle.

2. Heat to boiling. Cook, stirring several times, until rinds are soft, about 35 minutes.
3. Soften gelatin in ½ cup water. Stir gelatin and saccharin into hot mixture until saccharin dissolves. Seal in hot sterilized glasses. Store in refrigerator.

NOTE:
This jam should not be made in large quantities, for saccharin does not have the preserving qualities of sugar.

Orange-Pineapple Marmalade

Cooking time: 1 hour 10 minutes

Yield: 6 8-ounce glasses

- 3 large oranges, about 1 pound
- 3 cups water
- 2 cups fresh pineapple, diced
- 4 cups sugar
- ⅓ cup almonds, blanched and slivered

METHOD:
1. Use a sharp knife to cut the oranges in thin slices. Remove seeds, and tie in a piece of cheesecloth.
2. Put sliced oranges, seeds, and water in a kettle, let stand overnight.
3. The next day, cook mixture until peel is just tender, about 10 minutes.
4. Add pineapple and simmer 20 minutes.
5. Stir in sugar until dissolved. Bring to a boil.
6. Add nuts, reduce heat, and cook about 30 minutes.
7. Test for jell, and continue cooking another 10–15 minutes if necessary until set is obtained.
8. Remove from heat, remove cheesecloth, and cool about 1 hour. Stir well. Seal in hot sterilized glasses.

NOTE:
Very good as a glaze for pork, ham, and chicken. Try it in tea sandwiches with thin-sliced nut bread.

Scotch Orange Marmalade

Cooking time: 1 hour 30 minutes

Yield: 6 8-ounce glasses

2 large sweet oranges, about 1 pound
2 lemons, about ½ pound
1 grapefruit or 2 Florida thin-skinned
    oranges
    water
    sugar
    salt (optional)

METHOD:
1. Cut fruit into eighths, then use a very sharp knife or kitchen shears to cut fruit into fine slivers.
2. Remove the seeds, and put them in a measuring cup with ½ cup water. Let stand overnight.
3. Weigh the combined cut-up fruit. Add 6 cups water for each 1 pound of fruit. Let stand overnight.
4. The next day, strain the water from the seeds into the fruit. Simmer the fruit over low heat for 1 hour 15 minutes. Remove from heat, and cool to room temperature.
5. Measure the cooked fruit. Allow 2½ cups of sugar for each 2 cups (1 pint) of fruit. Stir in sugar.
6. Stir over low heat until sugar is completely dissolved, then bring to a rapid boil. Cook for about 10 minutes, and test for set. Cook an additional 5–10 minutes if necessary. Stir in ½ teaspoon salt, if desired.
7. Remove from heat, and stir well. Cool, stir again. Seal in hot sterilized glasses.

NOTE:
For a real "bite," reduce sugar to 2 cups per pint of cooked fruit. In cold weather, my breakfast specialty consists of real old-fashioned hot oatmeal topped with 2 or 3 spoonfuls of Scotch Marmalade. In any weather, a toasted, buttered English muffin and Scotch Marmalade is hard to beat.

Sweet Orange Marmalade

Cooking time: 1 hour 40 minutes

Yield: 5 8-ounce glasses

3 medium-size oranges, 1 pound
1 lemon
4 cups water
4 cups sugar
    dash salt

METHOD:
1. Finely cut or mince oranges, using a sharp knife, or chop in blender. Either way remove seeds.
2. Squeeze lemon, and reserve juice. Add lemon seeds to orange seeds, and tie in a piece of cheesecloth.
3. Combine chopped or slivered oranges, seeds, and water. Add squeezed out lemon halves. Let stand overnight. The next day, discard the lemon halves.
4. Simmer the mixture over low heat for about 1 hour 30 minutes, or until peel is soft. Remove bag of seeds, draining thoroughly before discarding.

5. Stir in lemon juice and sugar. Bring to a boil and cook rapidly for 8–10 minutes. Test for set.
6. If necessary, continue cooking an additional 8–10 minutes, or until setting point is reached.
7. Remove immediately from heat. Add a dash of salt, and stir briskly. Cool.
8. Stir cooled marmalade to distribute peel. Seal in hot sterilized glasses.

NOTE:

A great glaze for duck or ham. Spread or brush on during last 20 minutes in oven. And have you ever tried a toasted-cheese sandwich with an orange marmalade? So different and so good!

Peach-Cantaloupe Marmalade

Cooking time: 1 hour 30 minutes

Yield: 9 8-ounce glasses

> 4 cups ripe peaches, cubed
> 4 cups ripe cantaloupe, cubed
> 2 lemons, juice and grated rind
> 6 cups sugar
> ¼ teaspoon ground ginger

METHOD:
1. Layer the ingredients listed in a large bowl. Let stand overnight.
2. Turn into a large heavy kettle and cook slowly over low heat until very thick, about 1½ hours. Stir often to prevent scorching.
3. Let mixture cool to room temperature. Stir well to distribute ingredients. Seal in hot sterilized glasses.

NOTE:
Very pretty, very "peachy" in flavor. An unusual topping for ice cream or for hot baked desserts.

Peach Marmalade

Cooking time: 10 minutes

Yield: 6 8-ounce glasses

> 6 large firm peaches, about 2 pounds
> 7 cups sugar
> ½ cup fresh lemon juice
> 1 tablespoon butter or margarine
> 1 jar (1 pound) orange marmalade
> ½ bottle (3 ounces) liquid pectin

METHOD:
1. Peel, halve, and pit peaches. Put through a food grinder, using a fine blade.
2. Combine peaches, sugar, lemon juice, and butter in a heavy kettle.
3. Bring to a full rolling boil, cook 1 minute, stirring constantly.
4. Remove from heat, and stir in marmalade and pectin. Stir 5 minutes to keep fruit well distributed.
5. Skim. Seal in hot sterilized glasses.

NOTE:
For those who look for something different with peaches, swirl Peach Marmalade through plain or vanilla yogurt.

Peach-Macadamia Nut Conserve

Cooking time: 1 hour

Yield: 8 8-ounce glasses

8 medium-size peaches, about 2 pounds
1 orange
1 lemon
1½ cups seedless raisins
4 cups water
2 cups sugar
1 cup macadamia nuts, chopped

METHOD:

1. Peel, halve, and pit peaches. Cut into quarters. Grate orange. Squeeze orange and lemon. Tie orange and lemon seeds in a piece of cheesecloth.
2. Combine peaches, grated orange, citrus juices, seed bag, raisins, and water in a heavy kettle. Add sugar, and stir until sugar dissolves.
3. Heat to boiling. Cook, stirring often, until jam is thick and clear, about 1 hour. Remove seed bag. Stir in nuts. Cool. Seal in hot sterilized glasses.

NOTE:

This makes a delightful spread for layers of angel or sponge cake, garnished with whipped cream. Or drop a teaspoonful into tiny tarts for afternoon tea.

METHOD:

1. Halve and seed oranges. Cut oranges into thin slices. Tie seeds in a piece of cheesecloth. Combine oranges, seed bag, and water in a heavy kettle. Allow to stand overnight.
2. The next day add pineapple and bring to a boil, simmer for 40 minutes.
3. Stir in sugar until sugar dissolves. Add nuts. Cook until syrup tests for set, about 30 minutes. Remove seed bag.
4. Cool for 30 minutes. Seal in hot sterilized glasses.

NOTE:

This recipe can be made all year around. Just the right gift to bring over to welcome a new neighbor.

Pineapple Marmalade

Cooking time: 1 hour 30 minutes

Yield: 5 8-ounce glasses

3 oranges, about 1 pound
3 cups water
2 cups fresh pineapple, diced
4 cups sugar
¾ cup almonds, blanched and slivered

Quick Pineapple Marmalade

Cooking time: about 30 minutes

Yield: 3 8-ounce glasses

¾ cup brown sugar, packed
½ teaspoon ground cinnamon
1 slice lemon, minced
1 can (1 pound 13 ounces) crushed pineapple

METHOD:

1. Combine all ingredients.
2. Cook and stir over moderate heat until thick, about 30 minutes.
3. Seal in hot sterilized glasses. Keep in refrigerator.

NOTE:

Good served with cream cheese or cottage cheese. Makes a nice relish for pork or ham dishes.

Pineapple-Watermelon Marmalade

Cooking time: 4 hours

Yield: 10 8-ounce glasses

4 cups water
8 lemons, juice and grated rind
2 teaspoons ground ginger
rind of ½ large watermelon, about 4 pounds
1 large ripe pineapple, peeled, cored, and diced
8 cups sugar

METHOD:

1. Combine water, lemon rind and juice, and ginger in a large kettle. Bring to a boil, and cook 10 minutes. Skim.
2. Add the watermelon rind cut in small cubes. Simmer for 3 hours, stirring often.
3. Add the diced pineapple and the sugar. Stir until sugar is completely dissolved.
4. Bring to a rapid boil, reduce heat, and cook slowly for an additional 45 minutes.

5. Cool for about 1 hour. Seal in hot sterilized glasses.

NOTE:

Wonderful on pancakes or waffles. An excellent accompaniment to chicken or ham.

Plum Conserve

Cooking time: 45 minutes

Yield: 4 8-ounce glasses

1 can (1 pound 13 ounces) plums in syrup, pitted
½ cup seedless raisins
1 cup sugar
1 orange, chopped
1 tablespoon lemon juice
1 cup walnuts, chopped

METHOD:

1. Mix plums, raisins, sugar, and orange. Stir until sugar dissolves.
2. Bring to a rapid boil. Reduce heat to low, and simmer mixture until very thick, about 45 minutes. Stir often to prevent scorching.
3. Add lemon juice and walnuts, mix well. Seal in hot sterilized glasses.

NOTE:

The bittersweet flavor of Plum Conserve makes it a good relish with duck, pork, and turkey.

Rhubarb Conserve

Cooking time: 40 minutes

Yield: 12 8-ounce glasses

- 2 large oranges
- 2 large lemons
- 7½ cups cut-up rhubarb, about 2½ pounds
- 4 cups fresh red raspberries, about 1 pound
- 3 cups red currants, stemmed, about 1 pound
- 3 cups seedless raisins, chopped, 1 pound
- 10 cups sugar
- 4 cups walnuts or macadamia nuts, chopped, 1 pound

METHOD:

1. Halve, seed, and thinly slice oranges and lemons. Combine with rhubarb, raspberries, currants, raisins, and sugar in a heavy kettle.
2. Heat slowly to boiling, stirring constantly. Cook until mixture is as thick as jam, about 30 minutes.
3. Remove from heat. Stir in chopped nuts. Seal in hot sterilized glasses.

NOTE:

This is a particularly delicious jam to serve at a brunch.

Tangerine Marmalade

Cooking time: about 2 hours

Yield: 5–6 8-ounce glasses

- 4–5 medium tangerines, about 1 pound
- 3 cups water
- 3 cups sugar
- ½ teaspoon citric acid

  or

- 1 lemon, juice of

METHOD:

1. Cut tangerine peel in fine strips. Remove stringy white pith and seeds, tie in a piece of cheesecloth. Mash fruit segments.
2. Add water to peel, cheesecloth, and fruit pulp and let stand overnight in a heavy kettle.
3. The next day, simmer over low heat for about 1 hour 30 minutes, or until peel is tender. Remove bag of seeds, draining well.
4. Stir in sugar, and simmer a minute or two until it is completely dissolved. Stir in citric acid or lemon juice.
5. Bring mixture to a rapid boil, cook for about 20 minutes or until set is reached.
6. Remove from heat, cool. Stir well to distribute peel. Seal in hot sterilized glasses.

NOTE:

Tangerine Marmalade has an unusual flavor, much different from other marmalades. Spoon some over warm custard or pudding as a special sauce.

Three Fruit Marmalade

Cooking time: 1 hour 30 minutes

Yield: 6 8-ounce glasses

2 grapefruit, about 1 pound
2 large lemons, about ½ pound
4 sweet oranges, about 1½ pounds
  water
  sugar

METHOD:
1. Halve or quarter fruit, remove seeds, and put in ½ cup water. Let stand overnight.
2. Cut fruit in very thin slices. Weigh the fruit, and add 3 cups water to each pound of fruit. Let stand overnight.
3. The next day, strain the juice from the seeds into the fruit. Bring fruit mixture to a boil, reduce heat, and simmer about 1 hour 15 minutes, or until peel is tender. Cool.
4. Measure the cooked fruit. To each 2 cups of fruit, add 2½ cups sugar.
5. Stir mixture over low heat until sugar dissolves. Bring to a boil. Test for set at end of 10 minutes. Continue cooking an additional 5 minutes if necessary.
6. Cool. Stir to distribute peel. Seal in hot sterilized glasses.

NOTE:
This is a lovely marmalade to make during the winter when citrus fruits are at their best.

Tomato-Ginger Conserve

Cooking time: 1 hour 50 minutes

Yield: 15 8-ounce glasses

  2 lemons
  2 cups water
 15 medium-size ripe tomatoes, about 5 pounds
  6 large cooking apples, about 2 pounds
  6 cups sugar
  ½ teaspoon salt
  2 cups walnuts, chopped
1½ cups raisins
  ½ cup candied ginger, chopped

METHOD:
1. Quarter, seed, and cut lemons into very thin slices. Place in a heavy kettle with water.
2. Heat to boiling. Simmer until rind is soft, about 50 minutes.
3. Peel, core, and chop tomatoes and apples. Add to kettle with sugar and salt.
4. Heat, stirring often, until sugar dissolves. Cook, stirring and skimming often, 45 minutes. Add walnuts, raisins, and ginger to kettle. Cook, stirring several times, until syrup is thick and fruit transparent, about 15 minutes. Seal in hot sterilized glasses.

NOTE:
Excellent with sandwiches or served with fried shrimp.

Pickles and Relishes

The word "pickle" as defined in Merriam-Webster is a "brine or vinegar solution in which foods are preserved." Our Victorian forefathers used the word "pickle" to describe a small mischievous child, and even now we use the word "pickled" to describe a happy state of inebriation.

Pickles are known to have been used in Rome many centuries ago, and there is a reference to a sailor's salted provisions in the eleventh book of the Odyssey. Emigrants from many lands carried wooden kegs containing salted vegetables, meats, or whatever could be preserved, as their only "convenience foods." Settling in new lands, they continued to salt down whatever could be spared from frugal crops or whenever there was an abundance. This was their only way of preserving vegetables and fruits to see their families through the long, hard winters. There was no refrigeration as we know it, so salting or putting down in brine was a real life saver.

Vinegar (mostly from apples) was also used in pickling, and soon an enterprising medieval gourmet added the flavor of wild herbs to her salt and vinegar. In time, sugar was added and as spices became known and less expensive they also were used.

Thanks to the difficulties of the past and modern methods, we can enjoy many varieties of pickles today—sour, sweet-sour, sweet, spicy, and hot. I hope you will try many of these pickle and relish recipes, and enjoy each one.

The first rule is "read your recipe." Now that that's done, I am sure you have an urge to make some pickles. So let's get started.

Utensils

1. Glass jars: quart size (32-ounces), pint size (16-ounces), and half-pint size (8-ounces). And *new* rubber seals and screw caps.

2. Your preserving kettle: at least six-quart capacity, made of enamelware, aluminum, or stainless steel. (Copper, brass, iron, or galvanized utensils are apt to cause a bad color or flavor in your product.)

3. Another kettle or pan with a cover is also required, or a pressure canner. This is used for sterilizing your jars before using and for processing pickles in the water bath.

4. Glass, plastic, or china bowls for steeping overnight.

5. Two long-handled wooden or stainless-steel spoons. (Don't use plastic spoons as they might curl up in intense heat.)

6. Ladles: one small, one large.

7. Wide-mouth funnel for filling jars.

8. Chopping board; two if you have them.

9. Vegetable parer, knife for slicing, kitchen scissors.

10. Food chopper with medium and coarse blades.
11. Measuring spoons, and glass and metal measuring cups.
12. A grater.
13. A couple of strainers or colanders.
14. Some cheesecloth for your spice bags.

This looks like a formidable list. But most cooks have these utensils already in their kitchens. If not, try borrowing from some of your neighbors. They might even like to be invited in to share the cooking and the finished product. It's a wonderful way to make friends.

Hints for Making Pickles and Relishes

These short and simple directions apply to pickles and relishes, and also to chutneys. If you will commit them to memory, you should cook a healthy batch of pickles every time!

1. Use unwaxed cucumbers for pickle recipes.
2. White vinegar should be used for light-colored pickles, for relishes and chutneys. Cider or malt vinegar is best for darker-colored products.
3. Do not cut down on the amount of sugar or vinegar in any recipe, since sugar and vinegar are the preservatives. In fact, you may increase the vinegar or sugar by a small amount if you prefer the pickle or relish less thick and more sweet.
4. Some recipes call for coarse salt (also known as flake salt, kosher salt, dairy salt, or cheese salt), a grained sea salt with natural iodine and minerals. Coarse salt has a far more pronounced taste than ordinary salt. It is available everywhere. There is also a salt called pickling salt. Because it is a fine-grained, pure salt, it leaves no cloudy residue and thus is used when clear pickles are desired. However, pickling salt is not as easy to find as the coarse salt. (Do not confuse either coarse salt or pickling salt with what is called rock salt or ice-cream salt. The latter, sold for use in ice cream freezers, is coarse but very impure.)

5. Add about one quarter the amount of vinegar to the fruits or vegetables when first starting to cook, then add the rest during cooking. Putting in all of the vinegar at one time tends to take away too much of the natural flavors of the other ingredients.

6. Leave the lid off the kettle when using vinegar, and stir the mixture frequently.

7. In most recipes, pour the mixture into hot sterilized jars while it is still hot.

8. Process in a water bath if the recipe requires this step.

9. Store in a cool dry place, preferably in the dark, to keep well.

Water Bath for Your Pickles

A water bath is a method of processing foods at a temperature of 212 degrees to destroy the bacteria, enzymes, molds, and yeasts which can cause spoilage in acid foods. This is particularly true when you live in a warm climate.

Not every recipe in this section has to have a water bath. It depends upon the ratio between the natural acidity of the food and that of the pickling agent, such as vinegar or lemon juice, and also on the size of the jars used to pack the pickles. So, follow the specific directions in each recipe on use of the water bath.

Pickles are cooked in an open kettle and then packed into hot sterilized jars before going into the water bath. Precooking pickles eliminates shrinkage and an empty space that would result if the pickles were not cooked first. Follow individual recipe directions for packing jars with cooked pickles before placing in a water bath.

You need the following equipment for a water bath:

1. Your pickles, still hot, and packed in jars with lids and metal bands in place.

2. A deep, heavy aluminum kettle with a cover, or a pressure canner.

3. A wire basket or wooden rack to fit the bottom of kettle or canner.

4. A timer.

5. A pair of tongs to lift jars from pan.

If you are using a kettle for the water bath process, here are the specific steps to follow:

1. Fit wire basket or wooden rack into kettle.

2. Add hot water to half-fill the kettle.

3. Adjust the screw band on your jars with firm pressure all the way, then reverse a quarter turn back to allow for expansion during the boiling process.

4. Place the jars on rack in kettle, keeping them from touching each other.

5. Pour enough boiling water down the side of the kettle to cover the jars by two inches. Cover kettle.

6. Turn on heat, and when water comes to a boil, set a timer and continue to boil for the time given in the recipe. Add more boiling water, if needed, to keep the jars always covered by two inches of water.

7. When timer rings, turn off heat, remove jars carefully with tongs, place on towels away from drafts, and do not allow them to touch each other.

8. Tighten the screw bands on jars all the way and leave undisturbed for twenty-four hours.

You can also use a steam-pressure canner for your water bath, in which case you should observe the following steps:

1. Place jars on rack in pressure canner containing 2 inches of water. Leave room between jars for the steam to circulate freely.

2. Remove all the air in the pressure canner by letting the steam escape for 10 minutes before closing the petcock.

3. Count water-bath time from the moment the gauge registers the specific pressure given in the manufacturer's directions. Be sure to keep the pressure constant while processing.

4. When timer rings, slide pressure canner to another burner to cool. *Do not* open canner until the pressure gauge registers zero. Then open the petcock slowly until no more steam escapes.

Testing for Seal

After your pickles have cooled until they are cold, you should check each jar to see if it is perfectly sealed and completely airtight. To test a jar with a flat metal lid, press down in the center of the lid; if lid is drawn down, the jar is sealed. Or you can test for seal by tilting the jar and looking for leaks around the edges; if there is leakage, you do not have a perfect seal.

If seal is not perfect, you have three choices:

1. Eat up your pickles quickly.

2. Store pickles in refrigerator until used up.

3. Reprocess in a water bath in another hot sterilized jar with a new cap and a screw band.

Be sure to wipe all your jars and dry them thoroughly; label and date, then store in a cool, dark cupboard, with the temperature not above 60 degrees, for up to one year.

6. Remove spice bag. Spoon hot mixture into hot sterilized jars, and seal.

NOTE:

Barbecue Relish is wonderful to serve on hot dogs and hamburgers, and with cold meat sandwiches like roast beef.

Pickled Beans With Dill

Cooking time: 10 minutes

Yield: 4 16-ounce jars

- 2 pounds fresh green beans
- 4 cloves garlic
- 4 sprigs fresh dill
- 1 teaspoon red pepper
- 2 tablespoons coarse salt
- 4 cups white vinegar
- 4 cups water

METHOD:

1. Trim green beans to fit jars.
2. Divide prepared beans among hot sterilized jars. Add 1 clove garlic, 1 sprig dill, and ¼ teaspoon red pepper to each jar.
3. Heat salt, vinegar, and water to boiling in a large saucepan. Pour over beans in jars. Seal jars.
4. Keep 2 weeks or longer before using.

NOTE:

These beans will disappear in a jiffy when you serve them as hors d'oeuvres at your next party; calorie counters love them! Pickled Beans make a delicious vegetable course—warm or cold—and add a novel touch to salads.

Barbecue Relish

Cooking time: 50 minutes

Yield: 9 16-ounce jars

- 6 cucumbers, pared, seeded, and finely chopped, 2 pounds
- 6 onions, peeled and chopped, 2 pounds
- 8 green tomatoes, peeled and finely chopped, 2 pounds
- 3 large carrots, pared and finely chopped, 1 pound
- 3 sweet red peppers, halved, seeded, and finely chopped
- 1 green sweet pepper, halved, seeded, and finely chopped
- ½ cup salt
- 1½ cups sugar
- ½ cup mixed pickling spices, tied in cheesecloth
- ½ teaspoon cayenne pepper

METHOD:

1. Place prepared vegetables in a large bowl. Sprinkle with salt, and toss to mix well. Cover and let stand overnight.
2. The next day, drain liquid from salted vegetables and rinse well.
3. Combine sugar, vinegar, and spices in a heavy kettle.
4. Heat, stirring often, until sugar dissolves. Add drained vegetables.
5. Heat to boiling. Simmer 45 minutes.

Pickled Beets

Cooking time: 1 hour 30 minutes

Yield: about 3 16-ounce jars

- 3 pounds beets
- 1 teaspoon whole allspice
- 6 whole cloves
- 1 piece stick cinnamon
- ½ cup sugar
- 2 cups vinegar
- ½ cup water

METHOD:

1. Cook beets until tender in salted water in a large saucepan. Drain.
2. Remove beet skins by pressing skins gently with fingers under running cold water. If beets are very small leave whole; otherwise, slice or cube.
3. Tie spices in a piece of cheesecloth.
4. Heat sugar, vinegar, water, and spices to boiling in a heavy kettle.
5. Add prepared beets. Boil 5 minutes.
6. Remove spice bag. Spoon hot mixture into hot sterilized jars, and seal.

NOTE:

Pickled Beets are good in sandwiches and in salads, not to mention their popularity as a vegetable dish for summer and winter buffet parties. Save the juice from your beets, cover 6 shelled hard-cooked eggs with the spicy red liquid, and leave in a bowl overnight. Next day, remove eggs from liquid. Slice and serve on a platter with crisp celery and cubes of cheese, or slice and use in sandwiches, or as decoration for canapés.

Beet-Cabbage Pickle

Cooking time: 1 hour

Yield: 8 16-ounce jars

- 2 pounds large old beets
- 1 firm cabbage, about 2 pounds
- ⅓ cup sugar
- ½ teaspoon salt
- ½ teaspoon pepper
- 1½ cups water
- 1½ cups vinegar

METHOD:

1. Cook beets until tender in salted water in a large saucepan. Drain.
2. Remove beet skins by gently peeling skins with fingers under cold running water. Cube beets.
3. Quarter, core, and shred cabbage finely.
4. Combine all ingredients except vinegar in a heavy kettle.
5. Heat to boiling. Boil 5 minutes.
6. Add vinegar, and boil 5 minutes longer.
7. Spoon hot mixture into hot sterilized jars, and seal.

NOTE:

Good with fish and cheese dishes.

Blackberry Pickle

Cooking time: 35–40 minutes

Yield: about 4 16-ounce jars

- 8 cups blackberries, 2 pounds
- 4 cups sugar
- 2 tablespoons ground allspice
- 2 tablespoons ground ginger
- 2 cups white vinegar

METHOD:

1. Place blackberries in a heavy kettle with sugar and spices. Cover and let stand 12 hours or overnight.
2. Heat vinegar to boiling and pour over berries.
3. Heat berries to boiling, stirring often. Simmer 30 minutes.
4. Remove kettle from heat and allow mixture to cool.
5. Spoon into hot sterilized jars, and seal.

NOTE:

Nice with chicken, ham, and cheese.

Green Cabbage Pickle

Cooking time: 25 minutes

Yield: 10 16-ounce jars

- 1 large firm cabbage, finely shredded, about 3 pounds
- 4 large onions, thinly sliced
  coarse salt
- 6 cups vinegar
- 2 cups sugar
- 1 cup regular flour
- 2 tablespoons dry mustard
- 2 teaspoons curry powder

METHOD:

1. Layer cabbage, onions, and salt in a large earthenware or glass bowl. Cover bowl. Allow to stand for 24 hours.
2. The next day, drain vegetables very well in a colander. Rinse.
3. Combine vegetables and 4 cups vinegar in a heavy kettle.
4. Heat to boiling. Simmer 20 minutes, stirring several times.

5. Combine remaining 2 cups vinegar with remaining ingredients to make a smooth paste in a bowl.
6. Stir paste into cabbage mixture. Cook, stirring constantly, for 5 minutes. (If mixture becomes too thick, add a little water.)
7. Spoon into hot sterilized jars. Allow jars to stand overnight before sealing.

NOTE:
This Maori recipe from New Zealand is delicious served with roast lamb.

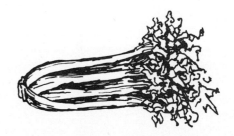

Celery-Pepper Relish

Cooking time: 15 minutes

Yield: 12 16-ounce jars

1 large bunch celery, trimmed and cut into ½-inch pieces
12 sweet red peppers, halved and chopped
12 hot green peppers, halved, seeded, and chopped
12 large green tomatoes, peeled and chopped
12 large onions, chopped
  boiling water
6 cups vinegar
2 cups sugar
¼ cup salt

METHOD:
1. Combine prepared vegetables in a very large bowl. Cover with boiling water. Allow to stand for 5 minutes. Drain.
2. Combine vinegar, sugar, and salt in a heavy kettle.
3. Heat to boiling. Add drained vegetables.
4. Boil 10 minutes, stirring occasionally.
5. Spoon into hot sterilized jars, and seal.

NOTE:
Sweet peppers are green at maturity, but turn red later and are found in food stores in both stages. Hot peppers, too, can be purchased green, yellowish green, or red, although they are used most generally in the red stage. Serve this relish with all cold meats.

Pickled Red Cabbage

Cooking time: none

Yield: 3 16-ounce jars

1 firm red cabbage, about 2 pounds
  coarse salt
  hot Spiced Vinegar (page 131)

METHOD:
1. Use a very sharp knife, or a shredder, to shred a firm cabbage head finely.
2. Sprinkle salt over the shredded cabbage, toss well to mix. Let stand 24 hours.
3. Turn cabbage into a colander, and drain thoroughly.
4. Pack the shredded cabbage in hot sterilized jars and add hot Spiced Vinegar to cover. Seal.
5. Allow to mellow for at least one week before using.

NOTE:
Great with corned beef.

Cherry Pickles

Cooking time: 50 minutes

Yield: 9–10 16-ounce jars

24 cups Bing cherries, about 6 pounds
4 tablespoons whole cloves
6 cups sugar
1 cup vinegar

METHOD:
1. Stem and pit cherries.
2. Tie whole cloves in a piece of cheese-cloth.
3. Combine cherries and remaining ingredients in a heavy kettle.
4. Heat to boiling. Simmer 45 minutes.
5. Remove spice bag. Spoon hot mixture into hot sterilized jars, and seal.

NOTE:
These pickles keep well and go well with roast chicken, duck, or pork.

Quick Pickled Cherries

Cooking time: 10 minutes

Yield: 5 16-ounce jars

2½ cups brown sugar, packed
1 cup cider vinegar
1 cup juice drained from cherries
2 teaspoons whole cloves
few whole allspice
6 2-inch sticks cinnamon
4 cans (1 pound each) sour red cherries, drained

METHOD:
1. Combine brown sugar, vinegar, cherry juice, and spices tied in a piece of cheesecloth.
2. Bring to a rapid boil. Reduce heat and cook 5 minutes.
3. Add cherries, and cook 5 minutes. Spoon immediately into hot sterilized jars, and seal.

NOTE:
Try this with duck, pheasant, quail, and other game birds.

Cherry Relish

Cooking time: none

Yield: 2 8-ounce jars

1 can (1 pound) dark sweet cherries, drained
1 medium-size orange
½ cup macadamia nuts or walnuts, chopped

METHOD:
1. Pit and chop cherries. Peel orange, and chop. Remove seeds.
2. Combine chopped cherries and orange with nuts in a bowl.
3. Place in a refrigerator for an hour to allow flavors to mellow.
4. Spoon into hot sterilized jars, and seal. Keep refrigerated.

NOTE:
Serve Cherry Relish with chicken, veal, pork, ham.

Christmas Relish

Cooking time: 40 minutes

Yield: 5 16-ounce jars

8 cups fresh cranberries, 2 pounds
1 onion, finely chopped
1 apple, peeled, cored, and finely chopped
1½ cups seedless raisins
3 cups sugar
1 cup chopped celery
1 cup water
1 piece stick cinnamon
1½ teaspoons ground ginger
¼ teaspoon ground cloves

METHOD:
1. Combine all ingredients in a heavy kettle.
2. Heat to boiling. Simmer 20 minutes or until berries pop.
3. Continue cooking, stirring often, until mixture thickens, about 20 minutes.
4. Spoon into hot sterilized jars, and seal.

NOTE:
Take along some relish to picnics, pot-luck suppers, or banquets. Serve with Christmas turkey.

Fresh Corn Relish

Cooking time: 40 minutes

Yield: 6 16-ounce jars

12 ears fresh corn, husks removed
1 small head cabbage, quartered, cored, and shredded
4 onions, peeled and chopped
3 sweet red peppers, halved, seeded, and chopped
2 cups sugar
3 tablespoons flour
1 tablespoon dry mustard
1 teaspoon turmeric or curry powder
4 cups white vinegar

METHOD:
1. Cook corn in salted, boiling water 3 minutes in a heavy kettle. Cool. Cut kernels from cobs.
2. Put cabbage, onions, and pepper through a food grinder, using a coarse blade.
3. Combine corn and ground vegetables in the same kettle.
4. Combine sugar, flour, mustard and turmeric in a large heavy saucepan. Stir in vinegar until smooth.
5. Heat to boiling. Pour over vegetables in kettle.
6. Cook, stirring frequently, 30 minutes.
7. Spoon into hot sterilized jars, and seal.

NOTE:
Take some of this to a picnic. Besides being pretty to look at, Fresh Corn Relish is the perfect topping for hot dogs and hamburgers.

Quick Corn Relish

Cooking time: none

Yield: 2 8-ounce jars

- 1 can (1 pound) whole-kernel corn, drained
- 4 tablespoons sweet pickle relish
- 1 tablespoon sweet red pepper, chopped
- ½ teaspoon prepared mustard
  mayonnaise to moisten
  pinch of garlic powder
      or
  small chopped onion
  salt to taste

METHOD:
1. Combine all ingredients in a bowl.
2. Allow to stand at room temperature for 30 minutes.
3. Spoon into hot sterilized jars, and seal. Keep refrigerated.

NOTE:
Serve as a relish or for hamburgers, meat loaf, or cold cuts.

Cranberry Relish

Cooking time: none

Yield: 4 8-ounce jars

- 4 cups fresh cranberries, 1 pound
- 2 lemons, sliced and seeded
- ¾ cup orange marmalade
- ½ teaspoon salt

METHOD:
1. Put cranberries and lemon slices through food grinder, using coarse blade. Place in a bowl.
2. Stir in marmalade and salt. Allow to stand 2–3 hours to blend flavors.
3. Spoon into hot sterilized jars, and seal. Keep refrigerated.

NOTE:
As a garnish, fill pear or peach halves with this relish. Serve on a platter with hot or cold turkey.

Cucumber Pickle

Cooking time: 35 minutes

Yield: about 9 16-ounce jars

- 16 small cucumbers, in quarter-inch slices
- 8 onions, peeled and sliced
- 2 sweet red peppers, seeded and sliced
- 2 green peppers, seeded and sliced
- ½ cup salt
- 3 cups sugar
- 5 cups vinegar
- 2 tablespoons mustard seeds, tied in cheesecloth
- 1½ teaspoon turmeric
- ½ teaspoon ground cloves

METHOD:
1. Layer prepared vegetables in a large earthenware or glass bowl. Sprinkle with salt.
2. Place a layer of chopped ice over vegetables and cover with a plate with a heavy weight on top. Let stand for 3 hours.
3. Drain and rinse pickles. Combine with remaining ingredients in a heavy kettle.
4. Heat, stirring often, to boiling. Simmer 30 minutes.
5. Remove spice bag. Spoon hot pickles into hot sterilized jars, and seal.

NOTE:
Serve with cold sliced beef or turkey, and any meat sandwiches.

Pickled Cucumbers

Cooking time: none
Water bath: 15 minutes

Yield: optional

fresh cucumbers
coarse salt
Spiced Vinegar (page 131)

METHOD:
1. Sprinkle cucumbers with coarse salt (not table salt). Let stand for 24 hours.
2. Wash salt off cucumbers in cold water, and pack into hot sterilized jars.
3. Fill jars with Spiced Vinegar until cucumbers are completely covered.
4. Cook in a water bath for 15 minutes.

NOTE:
If the cucumbers are very small, leave whole. If cucumbers are medium to large, cut into convenient pieces. A must with cold cuts.

Date Pickles

Cooking time: 10 minutes
Water bath: 15 minutes

Yield: 3 16-ounce jars

4 cups fresh dates, pitted, 2 pounds
½ cup mixed pickling spice, tied in a
**   piece of cheesecloth**
2¼ cups vinegar
¼ teaspoon salt

METHOD:
1. Divide pitted dates among 3 hot sterilized jars.
2. Combine spice bag with vinegar and salt in a saucepan. Heat to boiling. Simmer 5 minutes. Remove spice bag.
3. Pour over dates in jars. Seal jars.
4. Cook in a water bath for 15 minutes.

NOTE:
Keep for 3 months before using. Delicious with cream-cheese molds.

Dill Pickles

Cooking time: none
Water bath: 15 minutes

Yield: 4 16-ounce jars

6 cucumbers, 4 to 5 inches long
**   grape leaves, washed and rolled**
**   (optional)**
4 slices onion
8 sprigs fresh dill
2 teaspoons prepared horseradish
2 teaspoons mustard seeds, crushed
⅓ cup coarse salt
½ cup vinegar
5 cups water

METHOD:
1. Halve cucumbers, lengthwise. Pack 3 halves with grape leaves into each of 4 hot sterilized jars.
2. Divide the onion, dill, horseradish, and mustard seeds among jars.
3. Combine salt, vinegar, and water in a heavy saucepan.
4. Heat to boiling. Pour over cucumbers in jars. Seal jars immediately.
5. Cook in a water bath 15 minutes.

NOTE:
Keep 2–3 weeks before using. Try in long slices on a ham sandwich.

Shortcut Dill Pickles

Cooking time: 10 minutes
Water bath: 15 minutes
Yield: about 4 16-ounce jars

- **6 large dill pickles**
- **2 cups sugar**
- **½ cup vinegar**
- **1 cup water**

METHOD:
1. Wash pickles well, and cut into ½-inch slices.
2. Stir sugar, vinegar, and water in a heavy kettle until sugar dissolves.
3. Heat to boiling. Add sliced pickles, and simmer 5 minutes.
4. Pack hot mixture into hot sterilized jars. Allow to cool, then seal jars.
5. Cook in a water bath for 15 minutes.

NOTE:
Lovely to take on a picnic.

Pickled Eggs

Cooking time: few minutes
Yield: 4 16-ounce jars

- **16 hard-cooked eggs**
- **2 tablespoons whole allspice**
- **2 tablespoons whole peppercorns**
- **4 cups white vinegar**
- **2 tablespoons ground ginger**

METHOD:
1. Shell eggs. Pack into 4 hot sterilized jars.
2. Tie allspice and peppercorns in a piece of cheesecloth.
3. Heat vinegar, spice bag, and ground ginger to boiling in a large heavy saucepan. Simmer a few minutes.
4. Remove spice bag. Pour hot liquid over eggs in jars to cover completely.
5. Allow liquid to cool, then seal jars.

NOTE:
Pickled Eggs are a nice change from the usual deviled eggs. Have these on hand for church suppers and picnics, or to accompany a main-course salad.

Fig Pickles

Cooking time: 1 hour 10 minutes
Yield: 4 8-ounce jars

- **2 cups dried figs, 1 pound**
  cold water
- **2 cups brown sugar**
- **1 cup vinegar**
- **2 teaspoons ground cinnamon**
- **2 teaspoons ground cloves**
- **1 teaspoon ground allspice**

METHOD:
1. Wash figs in cold running water. Place in a bowl, and cover with cold water. Cover bowl with a towel. Allow to stand overnight.
2. The next day, drain figs in a colander.
3. Combine sugar, vinegar, and spices in heavy kettle.
4. Heat to boiling. Boil 10 minutes to make a good syrup.
5. Add figs. Simmer slowly for 1 hour.
6. Spoon into hot sterilized jars, and seal.

NOTE:

Delicious with pork, cold roast beef, ham, or cheese.

Pickled Fresh Fruits

Cooking time: 45 minutes

Yield: 4 8-ounce jars

2 pounds pears, peaches, plums, apricots or crab apples
1 cup vinegar
1 teaspoon mixed pickling spices
2 cups sugar

METHOD:

1. Peel, quarter, and core pears. Peel, quarter, and pit peaches. Halve and pit plums or apricots. If using crab apples, be sure they are free from bruises or blemishes, and use whole.
2. Combine vinegar and mixed pickling spices in a heavy kettle.
3. Heat to boiling. Simmer 10 minutes. Strain vinegar, and return to kettle.
4. Add sugar. Heat to boiling.
5. Add prepared fruit. Simmer gently 20 minutes or just until tender.
6. Divide fruit among 4 hot sterilized jars.
7. Boil syrup until thickened. Pour over fruits, and seal.

NOTE:

Serve any of these pickled fruits in place of green salad with hot or cold ham, pork, beef, or veal.

Ginger-Grape Relish

Cooking time: none

Yield: 6 8-ounce jars

3 green apples, peeled, quartered, and cored, about 1 pound
3 cups green grapes, stems removed, about 1½ pounds
3 onions, peeled and chopped, 1 pound
⅓ cup candied ginger, sliced
2 lemons
1½ teaspoons salt
2 cups fresh coconut, grated
   sugar (optional)

METHOD:

1. Put the apples, grapes, onions, and ginger through a food grinder, using a coarse blade. Place in a bowl.
2. Grate lemons, and squeeze. Add rind and juice to fruit mixture with salt.
3. Stir in coconut, and blend well. Taste, and add sugar if a sweeter mixture is desired.
4. Spoon into hot sterilized jars, and seal.

NOTE:

Allow to stand a few days to improve the flavor. Serve with curry dishes, chicken, and seafood.

Homestyle Pickle Slices

Cooking time: 50 minutes
Water bath: 15 minutes
                Yield: 10–11 16-ounce jars

12–15 medium-size cucumbers,
    thinly sliced
1½ pounds onions, thinly sliced
½ cup salt
3 cups water
1½ cups sugar
3 cups white vinegar
2 cloves garlic
2 teaspoons mustard seed
1½ teaspoons ground ginger
1 teaspoon turmeric.

METHOD:
1. Place sliced vegetables in a large crock.
2. Dissolve salt in water and pour over vegetables.
3. Place a large plate or wooden lid on top of vegetables to weight them down. Let stand 12 hours.
4. Place remaining ingredients in a heavy kettle. Heat to boiling.
5. Drain and rinse vegetables, add to boiling spice mixture. Simmer 45 minutes.
6. Remove garlic. Spoon hot pickles into hot sterilized jars, and cover with liquid to within ⅛ inch of top; be sure the contents of the jars are covered in the liquid. Seal jars.
7. Process in water bath for 15 minutes.

NOTE:
Serve with all cold meat, hamburgers, meat loaf, and frankfurters.

Indian Relish

Cooking time: 1 hour 40 minutes
                Yield: 8 16-ounce jars

3 cups mixed dried fruits (dates, prunes, raisins, pineapple, cherries, and/or citron)
1 can (1 pound 12 ounces) whole peeled tomatoes
1 can (1 pound 12 ounces) crushed pineapple
2 cloves garlic, minced
3 cups chopped onion
2 cups cider vinegar
2 cups brown sugar
16 whole cloves, tied in a piece of cheesecloth
4 pieces stick cinnamon
2 tablespoons chili powder
2 teaspoons ground ginger
2 teaspoons salt

METHOD:
1. Pit fruits, if necessary, and dice.
2. Combine diced fruits with tomatoes, pineapple, garlic, and onion in a heavy kettle. Stir in vinegar, sugar, salt and spice.
3. Heat slowly to boiling. Cover pan, and cook over very low heat for 30 minutes.
4. Uncover pan. Continue cooking, stirring occasionally, 1 hour, or until thick.
5. Remove spice bag. Cool completely. Spoon into hot sterilized jars, and seal. Keep refrigerated.

NOTE:
Serve with lamb curry, meat loaf, or fresh ham. Use for sandwiches or canapés.

Spark up picnic and patio menus with homemade Pickled Beans with Dill, Pickled Onions, Pickled Red Peppers, Pickled Mushrooms, Pickled Beets, Homestyle Pickle Slices, and Pickled Walnuts.

All-Vegetable Indian Relish

Cooking time: 30 minutes

Yield: 6 16-ounce jars

16 green tomatoes, about 4 pounds
16 ripe tomatoes, about 4 pounds
 3 sweet green peppers, halved and
   seeded
 3 sweet red peppers, halved and seeded
 1 cucumber
 7 cups chopped celery
 3 cups chopped onion
⅔ cup salt
 6 cups cider vinegar
 6 cups brown sugar, firmly packed
 1 tablespoon mustard seeds
½ teaspoon seasoned pepper
   (a blend of peppers)

METHOD:
1. Chop tomatoes, peppers, and cucumber in a food chopper, using a fine blade. Combine with celery and onions in a very large bowl; sprinkle with salt. Allow to stand 12 hours or overnight.
2. The next day, drain vegetables and discard liquid. Combine vegetables with remaining ingredients in a heavy kettle.
3. Heat to boiling. Simmer slowly, stirring several times, until thick, about 30 minutes.
4. Spoon into hot sterilized jars, and seal.

NOTE:
The family will want to spoon All-Vegetable Indian Relish over hamburgers or tuck it into the roll with frankfurters.

Kim Chee

Cooking time: none

Yield: 4 16-ounce jars

 1 fresh Chinese cabbage or celery cabbage
½ cup coarse salt
 2 scallions, finely chopped
 3 small cloves garlic, finely chopped
 3 tablespoons hot red peppers,
   finely chopped
 1 tablespoon sugar
 1 teaspoon green ginger, finely chopped
       or
½ teaspoon ground ginger
 4 cups water

METHOD:
1. Cut cabbage into 1½-inch lengths. Mix in salt, and add water to cover. Soak 4 hours.
2. Drain cabbage well. (It should be limp.) Combine cabbage with remaining ingredients.
3. Pack into hot sterilized jars, and seal.
4. Refrigerate for two days before using.

NOTE:
Kim Chee is a Korean recipe, used as a pickle or garnish. This pickle is strong smelling, so seal carefully. Otherwise the other foods in the refrigerator will pick up the flavor and odor.

Pickled Mushrooms

Cooking time: 12 minutes

Yield: 8 16-ounce jars

- **2 pounds small, fresh button mushrooms**
- **water**
- **¼ cup salt**
- **8 cups white vinegar**
- **2 teaspoons black pepper**
- **½ teaspoon ground mace**

METHOD:

1. Peel mushrooms, or rub off skin with a damp cloth dipped in salt.
2. Place mushrooms in a heavy kettle. Cover with water and add salt.
3. Heat to boiling. Boil for 5 minutes. Drain.
4. Pack into hot sterilized jars.
5. Combine vinegar and spices in a saucepan.
6. Heat to boiling. Pour over mushrooms in jars to cover completely, and seal jars.

NOTE:

Add Pickled Mushrooms to your braised beef, stews, or chops. A few go well in a green salad. Pickled Mushrooms are very popular served as hors d'oeuvres with cocktails before dinner.

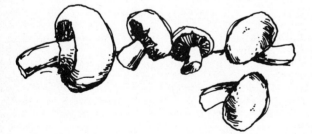

Mustard Pickle

Cooking time: 25 minutes

Water bath: 20 minutes

Yield: 8 16-ounce jars

- **1 small head cauliflower**
- **3 medium-size green tomatoes, about 1 pound**
- **2 medium-size zucchini, halved, about 1 pound**
- **2 medium-size cucumbers**
- **coarse salt**
- **4 cups vinegar**
- **½ cup dry mustard**
- **¼ cup curry powder or turmeric**
- **2 tablespoons flour**
- **½ cup sugar**

METHOD:

1. Separate cauliflower into florets. Cut tomatoes, squash, and cucumbers into thin slices.
2. Layer vegetables and salt in a large bowl. Cover bowl with a towel. Allow to stand overnight.
3. The next day, drain and rinse vegetables. Toss in a cloth to dry.
4. Blend 1 cup vinegar with dry mustard, curry powder, and flour to a smooth paste in a bowl.
5. Combine remaining 3 cups vinegar and sugar in a heavy kettle.
6. Heat to boiling. Boil for 5 minutes.
7. Add prepared vegetables. Cook 20 minutes. Stir in mustard paste, and cook 5 minutes longer.
8. Spoon into hot sterilized jars, and seal.
9. Cook in a water bath for 20 minutes.

NOTE:

This is a marvelous pickle for all meats.

Pickled Nasturtium Seeds

Cooking time: 15 minutes

Yield: 4 16-ounce jars

- 4 cups nasturtium seeds
  brine
- 4 cups vinegar
- 1 shallot or small onion, chopped
- 2 tablespoons ground mace
- 4 whole cloves

METHOD:
1. Rinse seeds well. Make a brine by dissolving ¼ cup salt in 4 cups water. Combine seeds and brine in a glass or pottery bowl, cover with a clean kitchen towel. Let stand 24 hours.
2. Drain seeds, rinse well. Repeat soaking procedure with fresh brine (see above). Let stand 24 hours.
3. Drain seeds, rinse well, and repeat soaking procedure for a third time. Let stand overnight.
4. Wash seeds thoroughly in cold running water, dry on paper towels. Divide among 4 hot sterilized jars.
5. Combine remaining ingredients in saucepan, heat to boiling. Simmer 15 minutes, skim.
6. Pour liquid over seeds. Allow jars to cool to room temperature before sealing.

NOTE:
Use these seeds in place of capers to decorate deviled eggs, canapés, or green salad. The seeds can be added to a white sauce, or chopped into mayonnaise and used as tartar sauce for fish.

Okra Pickles

Cooking time: 10 minutes
Water bath: 15 minutes

Yield: 6 16-ounce jars

- 3 pounds okra, uncut
- 6 sprigs fresh dill
    or
- 3 teaspoons dried dill
- 6 cloves garlic
  celery leaves
- ¼ cup coarse salt
- 4 cups vinegar
- 4 cups water

METHOD:
1. Rinse okra thoroughly. Pack into 6 hot sterilized jars.
2. Place a sprig of dill (or ½ teaspoon dried dill), a clove of garlic, and several celery leaves in each jar.
3. Heat salt, vinegar, and water to boiling in a large heavy saucepan. Simmer 10 minutes.
4. Pour hot liquid over okra to within ⅛-inch of top. Seal jars immediately.
5. Cook in water bath for 15 minutes.

NOTE:
Okra is a favorite of the South and will become popular with Northerners when cooked this way.

Pickled Onions

Cooking time: none

Yield: 5–6 8-ounce jars

2 pounds tiny white onions
8 cups water
½ cup salt
4 cups Spiced Vinegar (page 131)

METHOD:
1. Select tiny white onions—the smaller the better—and peel.
2. Cover onions with the water and salt and let stand 24 hours.
3. Drain and rinse onions. Pack in hot sterilized jars.
4. Pour hot Spiced Vinegar over onions to fill jars, and seal.

NOTE:
The smallest Pickled Onions are perfect to use in cocktails like martinis and gibsons. Larger onions go well with cold cuts, steaks, and hamburgers.

Orange Pickles

Cooking time: 1 hour 30 minutes–2 hours

Yield: 2 16-ounce jars

6 oranges
3 cups water
3 cups granulated sugar
2 cups white vinegar
1 teaspoon ground cloves
1 teaspoon ground mace
1 teaspoon ground cinnamon
1 teaspoon grated lemon rind

METHOD:
1. Peel oranges and cut into thick slices. Remove any seeds.
2. Combine orange slices and water in a large heavy saucepan.
3. Heat to boiling. Simmer until tender and clear, about 15 minutes. Do not drain.
4. Combine sugar and vinegar in a heavy kettle. Tie cloves, mace, cinnamon, and lemon rind in a piece of cheesecloth. Add to kettle.
5. Heat to boiling. Simmer 30 minutes. Remove spice bag. Add orange slices and liquid.
6. Simmer gently for 1 hour.
7. Pack into hot sterilized jars and seal.

NOTE:
Serve with roast duck, ham, pork, and chicken.

Pickled Red Peppers

Cooking time: 5 minutes

Yield: 4 16-ounce jars

10–12 sweet red peppers, 4–5 inches long,
    about 2½ pounds
    boiling water
  2 cups sugar
  2 cups white vinegar
  2 cups water
  8 cloves garlic
  4 teaspoons salad oil
  2 teaspoons salt

METHOD:
1. Stem and seed peppers. Pack into 4 hot sterilized jars. Cover with boiling water. Let stand.
2. Combine sugar, vinegar, and 2 cups water in a heavy saucepan.
3. Heat to boiling. Simmer 5 minutes.
4. Drain water from peppers. Add 2 cloves garlic, 1 teaspoon salad oil, and ½ teaspoon salt to each jar.
5. Pour boiling vinegar mixture over peppers to within ⅛-inch of top of jar. Seal immediately.

NOTE:
Nice to have on hand to go with dishes of leftovers. Chop a pepper and add to stews or to your favorite Mexican dish.

Pickled Green Peppers

Cooking time: 5 minutes

Yield: 4 16-ounce jars

  3 pounds sweet green peppers,
    halved and seeded
    boiling water
  2 cups sugar
  2 cups white vinegar
  2 cups water
  8 cloves garlic
  4 teaspoons salad oil
  2 teaspoons salt

METHOD:
1. Cut peppers into half-inch pieces.
2. Pack into 4 16-ounce hot sterilized jars. Cover with boiling water. Let stand.
3. Combine sugar, vinegar, and 2 cups water in a heavy saucepan.
4. Heat to boiling. Simmer 5 minutes.
5. Drain water from peppers. Add 2 cloves garlic, 1 teaspoon salad oil, and ½ teaspoon salt to each jar.
6. Pour boiling vinegar mixture over peppers to within ⅛-inch of top of jar. Seal immediately.

NOTE:
When peppers are in good supply in your supermarket or in your garden, pickle them for the long cold winter. Pickled Green Peppers go well with meat loaf.

NOTE:

Serve this with grilled steaks. Or are you planning a fondue party? Make yours a little different. Fill small bowls with an assortment of your homemade relishes and chutneys, and let the guests help themselves, dipping their bread cubes or meat or seafoods. Lots of color, variety and fun!

Sweet Pepper Relish

Cooking time: 1 hour

Yield: 10 16-ounce jars

- 12 sweet red peppers, halved, seeded, and chopped
- 12 sweet green peppers, halved, seeded, and chopped
- 1 small cabbage, quartered, cored, and shredded
- 4 medium-size onions, chopped
  boiling water
- 2 cups sugar
- 2 cups vinegar
- 2 tablespoons salt
- 1 tablespoon celery salt

METHOD:

1. Combine peppers, cabbage, and onions in a heavy kettle.
2. Cover with boiling water. Allow to stand for 5 minutes. Drain. Return to kettle.
3. Cover vegetables with boiling water. Allow to stand for 10 minutes. Drain.
4. Combine sugar, vinegar, and salts in same kettle.
5. Heat to boiling. Boil for 10 minutes. Add prepared vegetables.
6. Cook 40 minutes.
7. Spoon into hot sterilized jars, and seal.

Pineapple Pickles

Cooking time: 55 minutes

Yield: 3 16-ounce jars

- 1 fresh ripe pineapple
- 2½ cups brown sugar
- 1 cup cider vinegar
- 2 cups water
- 4 tablespoons whole cloves
- 1 piece stick cinnamon

METHOD:

1. Slice, peel, and core pineapple. Cut into one-inch cubes.
2. Combine sugar, vinegar, and water in a heavy kettle.
3. Heat to boiling. Simmer 5 minutes to make a syrup.
4. Tie spices in a piece of cheesecloth. Add spice bag and pineapple cubes to syrup. Cover kettle. Cook 45 minutes.
5. Divide pineapple cubes among 3 hot sterilized jars.

6. Boil syrup and spices 5 minutes longer. Pour over pineapple to top of jars. Seal immediately.

NOTE:

Goes nicely with sliced cold pork, a platter of sausages, or fried fish. Or add some to a chicken salad.

Pineapple Relish

Cooking time: 20 minutes

Yield: 4 8-ounce jars

    1 large pineapple
       water
    1 cup brown sugar, packed
    2 tablespoons butter
    2 tablespoons vinegar
    1 teaspoon curry powder
    ½ teaspoon salt
    ¼ teaspoon ground ginger

METHOD:

1. Slice, peel, and core pineapple. Cut into very small pieces. Place in a large heavy saucepan and cover with water.
2. Heat to boiling. Simmer 10 minutes, or until pineapple is tender. Drain all water from saucepan. Add remaining ingredients.
3. Heat to boiling, stirring constantly. Simmer, stirring often, 10 minutes.
4. Spoon into hot sterilized jars, and seal.

NOTE:

Serve with cold sliced pork or ham and with cheese sandwiches.

Quick Pineapple Relish

Cooking time: 5 minutes

Yield: 2 4-ounce jars

    1½ cups crushed pineapple
    ½   cup brown sugar
    2   tablespoons butter
    2   tablespoons vinegar
    1   clove garlic, minced
    1   teaspoon curry powder
    ½   teaspoon salt

METHOD:

1. Combine all ingredients in a large heavy saucepan.
2. Heat to a boil, stirring constantly.
3. Simmer, stirring constantly, until well blended, about 3 minutes.
4. Spoon into hot sterilized jars, and seal.

NOTE:

Serve with pork, ham, or cheese sandwiches.

Damson Plum Pickles

Cooking time: 25 minutes

Yield: 8 16-ounce jars

- 4 **pounds firm Damson plums**
- 1 **tablespoon whole cloves**
- 1 **stick cinnamon**
- 3 **pounds brown sugar**
- 1 **cup cider vinegar**

METHOD:
1. Wash plums and remove stems.
2. Tie cloves and stick cinnamon in a piece of cheesecloth.
3. Combine sugar, vinegar, and spice bag in a heavy kettle.
4. Heat to boiling, stirring frequently. Boil 10 minutes. Remove spice bag.
5. Add plums. Boil 10 minutes, being careful not to break the fruit when stirring.
6. Pack into hot sterilized jars. Pour hot syrup over plums to top of jar. Cool plums before sealing.

NOTE:
Serve with ham, chicken, or toasted cheese sandwiches.

Summer Squash Pickles

Cooking time: about 15 minutes

Yield: 4 16-ounce jars

- 4 **medium-size summer squash,**
  about 2 pounds
- ½ **cup coarse salt**
- ½ **cup sugar**
- 1½ **cups white vinegar**
- 3 **tablespoons dry mustard**
- 1 **tablespoon ground ginger**
- 1 **tablespoon curry powder**
- 6 **peppercorns**

METHOD:
1. Peel squash, halve, seed, and cut into half-inch cubes. Layer with salt in a large bowl. Cover bowl with a towel. Allow to stand overnight.
2. The next day, drain and rinse squash in cold water, and place in a heavy kettle.
3. Combine sugar, vinegar, and spices in a heavy saucepan.
4. Heat to boiling. Boil for 5 minutes, and pour over squash.
5. Heat to boiling. Cook 5 minutes or just until squash is tender but not mushy.
6. Spoon hot mixture into hot sterilized jars, and seal.

NOTE:
Zucchini can be substituted for summer squash in this recipe. Use Summer Squash Pickles to spark up leftovers. Pickles of all kinds make leftovers more exciting.

102

Green Tomato Pickle

Cooking time: 1 hour 10 minutes

Yield: 10 16-ounce jars

18 green tomatoes, about 6 pounds
6 large onions, about 2½ pounds
½ cup salt
6 cups cider vinegar
4½ cups brown sugar, packed
6 green peppers, seeded and chopped,
   about 1½ pounds
3 sweet red peppers, seeded and chopped,
   about ¾ pound
6 cloves of garlic, minced
1 tablespoon whole cloves
1 tablespoon whole allspice
1 two-inch piece stick cinnamon
1 tablespoon celery seed
1 tablespoon ground ginger
1 tablespoon dry mustard
1 tablespoon salt

METHOD:

1. Cut the tomatoes and onions into very thin slices. Sprinkle with ½ cup salt. Let stand overnight in an earthenware bowl, stirring once or twice.
2. The next day, rinse under cold running water. Drain.
3. In a heavy kettle combine vinegar and sugar. Bring to a boil.
4. Add green and red peppers and garlic. Cook 10 minutes.
5. Add tomatoes and onions, salt, and spices tied in a piece of cheesecloth.
6. Simmer for 1 hour, stirring often.
7. Ladle pickle into hot sterilized jars and seal immediately.

NOTE:

This is an up-to-date version of grandmother's piccalilli. It is delicious with ham, and I like it spooned onto a piece of buttered bread to eat out of hand.

Tomato Relish

Cooking time: 1 hour 5 minutes

Yield: 6 16-ounce jars

    12 large ripe tomatoes, peeled and sliced,
        about 4 pounds
     4 large onions, peeled and sliced, about
        1½ pounds
        salt
     6 red chili peppers
     2 cups vinegar
    2¼ cups brown sugar
     1 tablespoon curry powder
     1 tablespoon flour

METHOD:

1. Layer tomato and onion slices with salt in a large bowl. Cover bowl with a towel. Allow to stand overnight. Drain.
2. Place tomatoes, onion, and chili peppers in a heavy kettle. Add 1½ cups of the vinegar.
3. Heat to boiling. Boil 5 minutes.
4. Mix sugar, curry powder, and flour in a bowl. Stir in remaining ½ cup vinegar to make a smooth paste.
5. Stir paste into vegetables in kettle. Cook, stirring often, 1 hour.
6. Spoon into hot sterilized jars, and seal.

NOTE:

This is especially delicious on top of grilled hamburgers.

Pickled Walnuts

Cooking time: none

Yield: optional

    green walnuts in the husk
    wet brine (¼ cup coarse salt to 2 cups
        cold water)
    Spiced Vinegar (page 131)

METHOD:

1. Pierce the green walnuts several times, using a silver fork or a knitting needle.
2. Put walnuts in a heavy crock, cover with wet brine, and let stand 2–3 days, depending on size.
3. Drain nuts and spread in a cloth-covered tray.
4. Dry the walnuts in direct sun, moving and turning them every hour or so. The nuts will turn black in 2–3 days. If the sun is very hot and the air dry, the nuts will turn in about 24 hours.

5. Pack the nuts in 16-ounce sterilized jars and cover with cold Spiced Vinegar. Seal. Let mellow and ripen at least 1 month before using.

NOTE:

This recipe is only for those who own or have access to a walnut tree, for the nuts must be green, not ripe as bought in the store.

Pickled Walnuts are an unusual, delicious accompaniment to any cold meat.

Watermelon Pickles, Number I

Cooking time: 45 minutes–1 hour

Yield: 8 16-ounce jars

½ watermelon
½ cup salt
  cold water
5 cups sugar
3 cups vinegar
2 thin lemon slices
2 thin lime slices
5 pieces stick cinnamon
1 tablespoon whole cloves
1 tablespoon whole allspice

METHOD:

1. Slice watermelon. Cut pink flesh into cubes to use for fruit salad. Peel off green skin and discard. Cut watermelon rind into cubes, or for fancy pickles, cut into circles with small cookie cutter. (You will have about 3½ pounds or 10 cups.)
2. Combine rind with salt and 4 cups cold water in a large bowl. Cover bowl with a towel. Soak overnight.
3. The next day, drain watermelon rind. Cover rind with fresh water in a heavy kettle.
4. Heat to boiling. Simmer until tender, about 15 minutes. Drain.
5. Combine sugar, vinegar, lemon and lime slices in the same kettle. Tie spices in a piece of cheesecloth. Add to kettle.
6. Heat to boiling. Cook over medium heat 20 minutes, or until thickened and syrupy.
7. Add cooked rind, a cup at a time. Simmer slowly 20 minutes, or until rind is clean and glossy.
8. Remove spice bag. Spoon into hot sterilized jars, filling jars to top with syrup, and seal.

NOTE:

The other day, while poking around in a gourmet food store, I was shocked to see watermelon pickles, packed in a small, fancy jar, priced at more than a dollar. Ridiculous when they can be made so cheaply and easily! One can eat the fleshy melon part and then pickle the rind so that it's almost like having your cake and eating it too.

Watermelon Pickles, Number II

Cooking time: 40 minutes

Yield: 10–12 16-ounce jars

1 **watermelon (underripe)**
½ **cup salt**
6 **cups white vinegar**
  water
1 **cup sugar**
½ **teaspoon oil of cloves***
½ **teaspoon oil of cinnamon***
  red food coloring

METHOD:

1. Slice watermelon. Cut pink flesh into cubes to use for fruit salad. Peel off green skin and discard. Cut rind into cubes (you will have about 7 pounds or 20 cups).
2. Combine rind with salt and 4 cups of the vinegar in a large bowl. Cover with a towel. Soak for 2 hours.
3. Drain rind, and rinse in cold water.

* Oil of cloves and oil of cinnamon can be purchased at the drugstore.

4. Place rind in heavy kettle. Add water, just to cover.
5. Heat to boiling. Boil 10 minutes, or until cubes are tender, but firm. Drain, and return to bowl.
6. Combine remaining 2 cups vinegar, sugar, oil of cloves, oil of cinnamon, and a few drops red food coloring in a heavy saucepan.
7. Heat to boiling. Pour over rind. Cover bowl with a towel. Allow to stand for two days.
8. On third day, pour rind and syrup into kettle.
9. Heat gently, just to boiling.
10. Spoon into hot sterilized jars, filling jars to top with syrup, and seal.

NOTE:

Watermelon Pickles should be left a few weeks to mellow before use. Serve them in your nicest glass dish so they can be seen in their translucent splendor. They go well with all kinds of meat and fish dishes, and are very popular with youngsters.

Zucchini Pickles

Cooking time: about 15 minutes
Water bath: 15 minutes

Yield: 3 16-ounce jars

4–5 zucchini, about 2 pounds
  ½ cup coarse salt
  ½ cup sugar
1½ cups white vinegar
  3 tablespoons dry mustard
  1 tablespoon ground ginger
  1 tablespoon curry powder
  6 peppercorns

METHOD:

1. Rinse unpeeled zucchini, and cut into half-inch slices. Layer with salt in a large bowl. Cover bowl with a towel, and allow to stand overnight.
2. The next day, drain and rinse squash in cold water and place in a heavy kettle.
3. Combine sugar, vinegar, and spices in a heavy saucepan.
4. Heat to boiling. Boil for 5 minutes and pour over squash.
5. Heat to boiling. Cook 5 minutes, or until tender but not mushy.
6. Spoon hot mixture into hot sterilized jars, and seal.
7. Cook in a water bath for 15 minutes.

NOTE:

Sparkle up an everyday meal with tasty Zucchini Pickles, and be sure to take on picnics.

Zucchini-Onion Pickle

Cooking time: 10 minutes
Water bath: 15 minutes

Yield: 6 16-ounce jars

15 large zucchini, about 5 pounds
  3 large onions, about 1 pound
  4 cups white vinegar
  2 cups sugar
  2 tablespoons salt
  2 teaspoons celery seeds
  2 teaspoons turmeric
  1 teaspoon dry mustard

METHOD:

1. Rinse unpeeled zucchini and cut into ¼-inch slices. Cut peeled onions into thin slices. Place in a large bowl.
2. Combine vinegar, sugar, salt, and spices in a heavy kettle.
3. Heat to boiling. Pour over zucchini and onions in bowl. Allow to stand 1 hour, stirring occasionally.
4. Return vinegar liquid and vegetables to kettle.
5. Heat to boiling. Simmer 3 minutes. Divide zucchini and onions among 6 hot sterilized jars. Heat liquid to boiling, and pour into jars to ⅛ inch of top, being sure liquid covers vegetables completely. Seal jars immediately.
6. Cook in a water bath for 15 minutes.

NOTE:

Serve with any hot or cold meats.

Chutneys

Apple Chutney

Cooking time: 2 hours

Yield: 9–10 8-ounce jars

7–8 tart cooking apples, about 2½ pounds
  2 onions, peeled and chopped
  3 cups seedless raisins, 1 pound
2⅓ cups brown sugar
  2 cups canned tomato sauce
2–3 pieces of green ginger, chopped
        or
  1 tablespoon ground ginger
  2 tablespoons salt
  1 cup vinegar
  ½ lemon, juice of

METHOD:

1. Peel, core, and slice apples to make 8 cups or more.
2. Combine apples with other ingredients and mix well.
3. Bring mixture to a slow boil, reduce heat to low, and simmer gently for about 2 hours, stirring often. Remove ginger.
4. Seal in hot sterilized jars.

NOTE:

The spicy fruit condiment known as chutney originated in India. Chutney should be preserved in small jars because you don't eat a lot of it at one time, and don't want too much open at one time.

Serve Apple Chutney with chicken or seafood curry dishes.

Banana Chutney

Cooking time: 30 minutes

Yield: 6 8-ounce jars

  2 medium-size onions, chopped, ½ pound
  1 cup water
  1 cup brown sugar, packed
1½ cups seedless raisins
  2 teaspoons curry powder (more if
    you wish)
  1 teaspoon salt
  ½ teaspoon ground ginger
  ½ teaspoon ground cinnamon
  2 cups vinegar
  6 large ripe bananas, peeled and sliced,
    about 2 pounds

METHOD:
1. Combine onions and water in a large, heavy saucepan. Heat to boiling. Simmer until soft, about 10 minutes.
2. Add sugar, raisins, spices, and vinegar. Heat to boiling. Add bananas.
3. Cook, stirring often, over low heat until mixture thickens, about 20 minutes. Seal in hot sterilized jars.

NOTE:
Chutney is an excellent seller at fund-raising projects. Serve Banana Chutney with lamb or lobster curry, use in sandwiches, and with cold meats.

Carrot Chutney

Cooking time: 1 hour

Yield: 10 8-ounce jars

16 large carrots, about 4 pounds
    water
  2 oranges
  1 lemon
  4 cups sugar
  1 cup white vinegar
  2 tablespoons mixed pickling spices,
    tied in cheesecloth
  ¾ cup seedless raisins

METHOD:
1. Scrape and slice carrots. Combine with water to cover in a large saucepan. Cook until soft, about 30 minutes. Drain. Mash with a potato masher or ricer.
2. Peel oranges and lemon. Cut the peel of 1 orange and the lemon into tiny slivers. Seed and slice oranges and lemons.
3. Heat sugar, vinegar, slivered peels, and spice bag to boiling in a heavy kettle. Boil 5 minutes to make a syrup. Add mashed carrots, sliced oranges and lemon, and raisins. Cook, stirring often, until mixture thickens, about 30 minutes. Remove spice bag. Seal in hot sterilized jars.

NOTE:
Serve Carrot Chutney with grilled chops. Very good with a fish curry.

Date Chutney

Cooking time: 1 hour

Yield: 6 8-ounce jars

  2 cups chopped dates, 1 pound
  9 large cooking apples, peeled, cored,
    and chopped, 3 pounds
  3 large onions, chopped, 1 pound
  4 cups vinegar
  1 tablespoon ground ginger
  1 teaspoon ground cloves
    dash of cayenne

METHOD:
1. Combine all ingredients in a heavy kettle.
2. Heat to boiling. Cook, stirring often, until mixture thickens, about 1 hour. Seal in hot sterilized jars.

NOTE:
You may want to increase the ginger a little for a more Indian-style chutney. This is delightful with a cheese omelet.

Mango Chutney, Number II

Cooking time: 2 hours

Yield: 10 8-ounce jars

4⅔ cups brown sugar
1½ cups cider vinegar
4 teaspoons ground ginger
½ teaspoon salt
¼ teaspoon garlic powder
1 teaspoon crushed red-pepper flakes
1 sweet green pepper, seeded and chopped
1 large sweet onion, peeled and chopped
5 large mangoes, peeled, pitted, and diced, about 5 pounds
2 large ripe tomatoes, peeled and chopped, 1 pound
2 cups seedless raisins

METHOD:

1. Combine brown sugar, vinegar, spices, green pepper, and onion in heavy kettle. Stir over low heat until sugar dissolves.
2. Add the diced mangoes, tomatoes, and raisins.
3. Cook over low-medium heat about 2 hours, or until thick. Stir frequently to prevent mixture sticking or scorching.
4. Cool. Seal in hot sterilized jars.

NOTE:

Very good with lamb curry. Or serve chilled with chicken salad.

Mango Chutney, Number I

Cooking time: 1 hour 30 minutes

Yield: 6 8-ounce jars

3 firm mangoes, about 3 pounds
1 cup coarse or flake salt
6 cups sugar or raw sugar
3 cups vinegar
6 cups seedless raisins, 2 pounds
½ cup minced ginger root
     or
2 tablespoons ground ginger
3 tablespoons minced garlic
4 small hot red peppers, seeded and chopped

METHOD:

1. Peel, pit, and slice mangoes. Layer with salt in a large bowl. Cover with a towel. Allow to stand overnight. Drain mango slices in a colander. Rinse.
2. The next day, combine sugar and vinegar in a heavy kettle. Heat to boiling. Simmer 30 minutes.
3. Add mango slices, raisins, ginger, garlic, and peppers. Simmer until mango slices are tender, about 1 hour. Seal in hot sterilized jars.

NOTE:

In Hawaii friends going on a visit take a box or bagful of mangoes when the crop is plentiful. Mangoes make wonderful pies, sauces, and puddings, and superb chutneys.

Blossom's Mango Chutney

Cooking time: 1 hour

Yield: 20 16-ounce jars

10 firm mangoes, about 10 pounds
¾ cup salt
10 cups sugar
6 cups cider vinegar
2 large onions, chopped
8 small red peppers, seeds removed and chopped
⅔ cup preserved ginger, thinly sliced
2 cloves garlic, minced
6 cups seedless raisins, 2 pounds
2 cups mixed candied fruits, 1 pound
1 cup almonds, sliced, or macadamia nuts, chopped

METHOD:
1. Peel, pit, and slice mangoes. Layer with salt in a large bowl. Cover with a towel. Allow to stand overnight. Drain mango slices in colander. Rinse.
2. The next day, combine sugar and vinegar in a heavy kettle.
3. Heat to boiling. Boil 5 minutes. Add drained mangoes, onions, red peppers, ginger, and garlic.
4. Cook 45 minutes, stirring often. Add raisins and candied fruits. Cook 15 minutes longer, stirring often.
5. Remove from heat. Stir in nuts and mix well.
6. Seal in hot sterilized jars.

NOTE:
Blossom's Mango Chutney improves with keeping and has a wonderful flavor. Good with curry, with all meats, and as a sandwich spread. A sure seller at any fund-raising project.

Orange Chutney

Cooking time: about 1 hour

Yield: 6 8-ounce jars

4 medium oranges, about 1 pound
1 medium onion, chopped
2 tart firm apples, cored, peeled, and chopped
¼ cup preserved ginger, finely chopped
1 small chili pepper, seeded and chopped
2 cups cider vinegar
1 cup raisins
2 tablespoons salt
1 cup brown sugar, packed

METHOD:
1. Thinly peel oranges, chop peel. Discard all white pith and seeds. Chop pulp.
2. Combine orange peel and pulp with remaining ingredients, and mix well.
3. Cook, and stir over low heat for about 1 hour, or until fruit is tender and mixture thick.
4. Seal in hot sterilized jars.

NOTE:
Serve with curry and pork dishes, roast veal and roast duck.

Pineapple Chutney

Cooking time: 55–60 minutes

Yield: 5 8-ounce jars

- 1 can (1 pound 13 ounces) crushed pineapple
- 2⅓ cups brown sugar
- 1 cup seedless raisins
- 1 tablespoon onion, minced
- 1 cup dates, diced
- ⅛ teaspoon pepper
- ½ teaspoon ground cloves
- ½ teaspoon ground cinnamon
- ½ teaspoon ground allspice
- ¼ teaspoon garlic powder
- 1 teaspoon salt
- 1 cup cider vinegar

METHOD:
1. Combine all ingredients and mix well.
2. Cook, and stir over low heat for 55–60 minutes or until very thick.
3. Cool. Seal in hot sterilized jars.

NOTE:
Spread this chutney on thin slices of boiled ham. Roll up and chill. Serve with salad for brunch or supper.

Hawaiian Pineapple Chutney

Cooking time: about 1 hour

Yield: 6 8-ounce jars

- 1 large ripe pineapple
- 1½ cups vinegar
- 1½ cups light brown sugar
- 2 tablespoons green ginger, minced
  - or
- 1 teaspoon ground ginger
- 4 cloves garlic, minced
- 1 tablespoon salt
- 1 large mild onion, chopped
- 1 cup golden raisins
- 2 red chili peppers, seeded and chopped
- 1 cup macadamia nuts, chopped

METHOD:
1. Slice, peel, core, and chop pineapple. You should have about 4–5 cups, depending on the size of the pineapple.
2. Combine pineapple, vinegar, sugar, ginger, garlic, and salt. Simmer over low heat for about 35 minutes, or until pineapple is tender.
3. Cook chopped onion in water to cover in a small saucepan for 5 minutes. Drain.
4. Add onion and remaining ingredients to pineapple mixture.
5. Cook, and stir over moderate heat until thick, about 20–25 minutes.
6. Seal in hot sterilized jars.

NOTE:
Serve this chutney with roast pork and pork chops.

Rhubarb Chutney

Cooking time: 25 minutes

Yield: 4–5 8-ounce jars

- 2 pounds fresh rhubarb*
- 1 cup dark corn syrup
- 1 cup cider vinegar
- 2 teaspoons cinnamon
- ½ teaspoon ground ginger
- ½ teaspoon ground cloves

METHOD:

1. Peel rhubarb, cut in small pieces.
2. Combine all ingredients, mix well. Bring to a boil, stirring all the time.
3. Reduce heat to moderate, cook until thick and smooth, about 25 minutes. Stir frequently to prevent scorching.
4. Seal in hot sterilized jars.

NOTE:

A new and different flavor with chutneys. Let it mellow at least two weeks before using. Then try it as a relish with tuna salad.

*Frozen rhubarb may be used if fresh is out of season. Frozen rhubarb comes cut up in 10-ounce packages. It should be partially defrosted before use in this recipe.

Plum Chutney

Cooking time: 45 minutes

Yield: 8 8-ounce jars

- 1 cup sugar
- ¾ cup vinegar
- ¾ cup water
- ½ teaspoon salt
- 3 pieces stick cinnamon
- ½ teaspoon cracked ginger
  - or
- 1 teaspoon ground ginger
- ½ teaspoon whole allspice
- ½ teaspoon whole cloves
- 36 prune plums, about 3 pounds
- 2 large apples, peeled, cored, and diced
- 1 cup seedless raisins
- ¼ cup instant minced onion

METHOD:

1. Combine sugar, vinegar, water, and salt in a heavy kettle. Tie spices in a piece of cheesecloth and add to kettle.
2. Heat to boiling. Simmer 5 minutes. Quarter and pit plums. Add to syrup with chopped apple, raisins, and onion.
3. Cook, stirring often, over low heat, until mixture thickens, about 40 minutes. Remove spice bag. Seal in hot sterilized jars.

NOTE:

Prune plums, also called Italian plums, are small and are generally blue-purple in color. Store this chutney at least 6 weeks before serving, then serve with ham, chicken, pork, and duck.

Red Tomato Chutney, Number I

Cooking time: about 1 hour

Yield: 8–9 8-ounce jars

- 12 ripe tomatoes, 4 pounds
- 3–4 tart green apples, cored and quartered, about 1 pound
- 2½ cups cider vinegar
- 2⅓ cups brown sugar
- 3 onions, sliced
- 1 tablespoon mustard seeds, crushed
- ¼ teaspoon cayenne pepper
- 2 tablespoons salt
- 1 tablespoon ground ginger

METHOD:

1. Use a wooden spoon to mash tomatoes in a large kettle.
2. Add remaining ingredients and mix well. Cook about 1 hour, or until mixture is soft and pulpy.
3. Let cooked mixture stand for 24 hours.
4. Force mixture through a coarse sieve.
5. Seal in hot sterilized jars.

NOTE:

Good in omelets or as a sandwich spread.

Red Tomato Chutney, Number II

Cooking time: 40 minutes

Yield: 4–5 8-ounce jars

- 5–6 ripe tomatoes, about 2 pounds
- 1 cup vinegar
- 1 cup brown sugar, packed
- 2 shallots or 1 small white onion, chopped
- ¼ teaspoon cayenne pepper
- ½ teaspoon garlic powder
- 4 tablespoons salt
- ¼ teaspoon ground ginger
- 1 tart green apple, peeled, cored, and chopped
- 1½ cups seedless raisins

METHOD:

1. Put tomatoes on a cookie sheet, or in a shallow pan, bake in a slow oven, 250 degrees, for 10 minutes, or until skins crack. Put through a coarse sieve.
2. Combine tomato pulp, vinegar, sugar, chopped shallots or onions, and seasonings. Mix well and bring to a boil.
3. Stir in apple and raisins. Cook for 30 minutes, stirring often.
4. Let stand overnight.
5. The next day, seal in hot sterilized jars.

NOTE:

A good chutney for pizza pies, or add it to a meat loaf for a different flavor.

These delicacies are tasty, colorful additions to every lunch, dinner, or supper. Pictured clockwise: Preserved Kumquats, Cranberry Relish, Watermelon Pickles, Spiced Cantaloupe, Sweet Pepper Relish, and Mango Chutney.

Green Tomato Chutney

Cooking time: 3 hours 20 minutes

Yield: 10–12 8-ounce jars

- 32 firm green tomatoes, about 8 pounds
- 1 tablespoon peppercorns
- 1 tablespoon mixed pickling spice
- ½ clove garlic
- 1 cup brown sugar, packed
- 2 tablespoons salt
- 1 cup vinegar
- 3 tart green apples, peeled, cored, and sliced, about 1 pound
- ¾ cup onion, chopped
- ¾ cup golden raisins
- ¾ cup granulated sugar
- ½ cup water

METHOD:

1. Core and quarter tomatoes. Combine with spices, garlic, brown sugar, salt, and vinegar.
2. Boil for 15–20 minutes, until tomatoes are soft. Put through a coarse sieve.
3. Return sieved mixture to kettle, and simmer over low heat for about 3 hours. Stir occasionally to prevent scorching.
4. Meanwhile, combine apples, onion, raisins, granulated sugar, and water in a large, heavy saucepan. Cook over moderate heat for about 15 minutes until apple slices are tender.
5. When tomato mixture is cooked, stir in apple mixture.
6. Seal in hot sterilized jars.

NOTE:

Green Tomato Chutney makes a tangy spread for cheese sandwiches. And try it with hamburgers or a cold-meat platter.

Turnip Chutney

Cooking time: 1 hour 30 minutes

Yield: 10 8-ounce jars

- 1 large yellow turnip, about 2 pounds
  water
- 1 tablespoon turmeric or curry powder
- 1 teaspoon dry mustard
- 4 cups cider vinegar
- 3 large cooking apples, peeled, cored, and chopped, 1 pound
- 3 large onions, finely chopped, 1 pound
- 1½ cups seedless raisins
- 1 cup brown sugar, packed
- 2 tablespoons salt
- ¼ teaspoon pepper

METHOD:

1. Slice, peel, and cube turnip. Combine with water to cover in a large saucepan. Cook until soft, about 30 minutes. Drain. Mash with a potato masher or ricer.
2. Blend turmeric and mustard with a little of the vinegar to make a smooth paste in the bottom of a heavy kettle. Add mashed turnips, apples, onions, raisins, sugar, salt, and pepper, and remaining vinegar.
3. Heat to boiling. Cook, stirring often, until mixture thickens, about 1 hour. Seal in hot sterilized jars.

NOTE:

Turnip Chutney is marvelous with corned beef.

Fruit Syrups and Juices

Blackberry Syrup

Cooking time: 15 minutes
Water bath: 10 minutes

Yield: 8 16-ounce jars

- **24 cups ripe blackberries, 6 pounds**
- **10 cups sugar**
- **3 cups water**

METHOD:

1. Mash the berries with a wooden spoon.
2. Heat sugar and water to boiling in a heavy kettle. Simmer for 10 minutes. Add mashed blackberries.
3. Heat to boiling and cook for 5 minutes over low heat. Sieve and pour into hot sterilized jars. Seal. Cook in a water bath for 10 minutes.

NOTE:

Ice cream never tastes better than when it is topped with this syrup.

Scandinavian Fruit Syrup

Cooking time: 3 minutes

Yield: 4 8-ounce jars

- 2 cups orange, pineapple, cranberry or grape juice
- 2 cups water
- 1 tablespoon arrowroot

  or
- 2 tablespoons cornstarch

  cold water

METHOD:

1. Heat fruit juice and water to a boil in a large saucepan.
2. Blend arrowroot with 2 tablespoons cold water. Stir into boiling liquid. Cook, stirring constantly, until mixture is smooth and clear, about 3 minutes. Pour into hot sterilized jars, and seal.

NOTE:

For the little ones who won't drink milk without a fuss, add 1 tablespoon of this fruit syrup to ½ pint of milk, put into a blender, and serve cold and frothy with a colored straw.

Ginger Beer, Number I

Cooking time: none

Yield: 6 32-ounce bottles

- 2 lemons
- 1 cup grated fresh ginger root

  or
- ⅓ cup ground ginger
- 8 cups sugar
- ½ cup cream of tartar
- 16 quarts boiling water
- 2 packages fresh brewer's yeast

METHOD:

1. Peel lemons and squeeze juice. Add peel and juice, ginger, sugar, and cream of tartar in a very large container. Pour boiling water over mixture.
2. Cool to lukewarm. Blend in yeast. Allow to stand overnight.

3. Skim off yeast, strain liquid. Pour into hot sterilized bottles, and cork. Store for at least 2 weeks before using.

NOTE:

Ginger Beer can add a Victorian touch to your next party. The bottles and corks can be purchased at a regular glass supplier; look up under "Glass" in telephone book.

Ginger Beer, Number II

Cooking time: none

Yield: 12 16-ounce bottles

- 4 cups sugar
- 4 lemons, juice of
- 24 cups cold water
- 2 teaspoons ground ginger
- 1 teaspoon tartaric acid

  Sultana raisins

METHOD:

1. Combine sugar, lemon juice, cold water, ground ginger, and tartaric acid in a very large bowl.
2. Stir until sugar dissolves. Strain into hot sterilized bottles. Add 3 Sultana raisins to each bottle. Cork bottles.

NOTE:

When the raisins rise to the top, in 3–4 days, Ginger Beer is ready.

Grape Juice

Cooking time: 45 minutes
Water bath: 10 minutes

Yield: 6 16-ounce jars

  10 cups Concord grapes, stemmed,
        about 5 pounds
   2 cups water
 1½ cups sugar

METHOD:

1. Combine grapes and water in a heavy kettle. Cover.
2. Heat very slowly to boiling. Cook, slowly, until very tender, about 30 minutes. Remove from heat. Place in a jelly bag, and let drip overnight.
3. The next day, combine grape juice and sugar in a heavy kettle. Heat to boiling. Seal in hot sterilized jars. Cook in a water bath for 10 minutes.

NOTE:

Serve chilled Grape Juice at breakfast, lunch, dinner, and in-between meals. Grape Juice is an excellent beverage to serve sick people, because it is tasty and rich in iron.

Lemon Syrup

Cooking time: 15 minutes

Yield: 3 16-ounce jars

 1 large lemon
 3 cups water
 4 cups sugar
 2 tablespoons citric acid

METHOD:

1. Peel lemon rind very thinly, and remove any white pith. Squeeze juice.
2. Heat lemon peel, juice, and water to boiling in a heavy saucepan. Simmer 10 minutes. Strain.
3. Combine strained liquid, sugar, and citric acid in same saucepan. Heat to boiling and simmer for 5 minutes.
4. Pour into hot sterilized jars. Seal when cool.

NOTE:

Use a few drops of Lemon Syrup in colas or other soft drinks for extra zip.

Pineapple Syrup

Cooking time: none

Yield: 6 8-ounce jars

 1 large ripe pineapple
 4 cups boiling water
 2 cups sugar

METHOD:

1. Slice, peel, and core pineapple. Chop into small pieces. Place in large bowl, cover with boiling water. Allow to stand for 2 days.
2. Strain liquid into a large saucepan. Stir in sugar until it dissolves. Heat to boiling.
3. Pour into hot sterilized jars. Seal when cold. Keep 1 week before using.

NOTE:

You can make great pineapple milkshakes and sodas at home with this syrup. It also goes well with ice cream and sherbets. Try it with waffles and pancakes.

Raspberry Syrup

Cooking time: 20 minutes
Water bath: 10 minutes

Yield: 6 16-ounce jars

8 cups red raspberries, 2 pounds
6 cups white vinegar
9 cups sugar

METHOD:
1. Place 4 cups raspberries in a large bowl. Cover with vinegar. Cover bowl. Allow to stand for 3 days.
2. Strain juice, and return to bowl with remaining 4 cups raspberries. Cover bowl. Allow to stand for 3 days.
3. Drain juice into a heavy kettle and add sugar.
4. Heat to boiling. Simmer slowly until syrupy, about 20 minutes. Cool. Seal in hot sterilized jars. Cook in a water bath for 10 minutes.

NOTE:
This syrup provides an excellent base for a party punch. It also helps to make milk palatable to children who normally dislike it. And, of course, it is heavenly poured over everything from ice cream to pancakes.

Raisin Nectar

Cooking time: none

Yield: 8 16-ounce jars

16 cups water
1 box (1 pound) raisins
4 cups sugar
3 lemons, juice of

METHOD:
1. Boil water for 5 minutes. Pour into a very large bowl and allow to become cold.
2. Add raisins, sugar, and lemon juice, and stir well. Allow to stand, stirring often, for 4 days, keeping bowl covered.
3. Strain liquid into hot sterilized jars, and seal.

NOTE:
Raisin Nectar will be ready in 14 days. Use as a topping on pound cake, custards, tapioca pudding, or to give fruit cocktail a new flavor.

Strawberry Syrup

Cooking time: 20 minutes
Water bath: 10 minutes

Yield: 4 16-ounce jars

6 cups ripe strawberries, hulled,
about 2 pounds
4 cups sugar

METHOD:
1. Mash the berries with a wooden spoon in a large bowl. Allow to stand for 24 hours. Strain strawberry juice into a heavy saucepan. Add sugar.
2. Heat to boiling. Simmer slowly, about 20 minutes until syrupy. Cool. Seal in hot sterilized jars. Cook in a water bath for 10 minutes.

NOTE:
Serve Strawberry Syrup with cheesecake, ice cream, pancakes, French toast, waffles, yogurt, or cooked or dry breakfast cereals.

Sauces

Governor's Sauce

Cooking time: 1 hour 30 minutes

Yield: 5 16-ounce jars

- 12 pounds green tomatoes, chopped, about 3 pounds
- 12 white onions, peeled and sliced, about 1 pound
- 1 cup salt
- 2¼ cups brown sugar
- 1½ teaspoons white pepper
- 1 teaspoon crushed red pepper flakes (optional)
- 2 teaspoons ground cloves
- 1½ teaspoons dry mustard
  cider vinegar

METHOD:

1. Make alternate layers of tomatoes, salt, and onions, making salt last layer. Let stand overnight.
2. The next day, drain mixture, and rinse thoroughly in cold running water.
3. Combine all ingredients in a heavy kettle, and add enough vinegar just to cover mixture. Cook over moderate heat until soft. Stir often to prevent scorching.
4. Cool mixture for an hour or so, then put through a sieve or process in a food mill.
5. Seal in hot sterilized jars.

NOTE:

Great with cold sliced beef and tongue. Add a little to mayonnaise for a very special salad dressing.

Horseradish Sauce

Cooking time: none

Yield: ½ cup

- ¼ cup fresh horseradish, grated
  or
- ¼ cup prepared horseradish, drained
- 1 teaspoon sugar
- 2 teaspoons prepared mustard
- 1 tablespoon heavy cream
  white vinegar
  salt and pepper

METHOD:

1. Mix horseradish, sugar, mustard, and heavy cream. Let stand for ½ hour.
2. Stir in vinegar until sauce is the consistency of heavy cream. Season with salt and pepper.
3. Spoon sauce into a jar or refrigerator container. Keep under refrigeration. This sauce is best made in small quantities, but you can double the recipe if more sauce is desired.

NOTE:

Serve with hot or cold roast beef or ham. Good with cold lamb, too.

Hot Sauce, Number I

Cooking time: 10 minutes

Yield: 2 cups

- ¼ cup garlic cloves, minced
- ¼ cup fresh horseradish, grated
  or
- ¼ cup prepared horseradish, drained
- ½ cup malt vinegar
- 1 teaspoon celery seed
- 1 2-inch cinnamon stick
  dash cayenne pepper
- ¾ cup soy sauce
- 2 tablespoons brown sugar
  vinegar

METHOD:

1. Combine garlic, horseradish, malt vinegar, and spices in a saucepan, and bring to a boil. Cool. Strain.
2. Stir in soy sauce, sugar, and enough vinegar (use vinegar from pickled walnuts or onions) to fill 1 pint jar. Seal, and keep in refrigerator to be used as needed.

NOTE:

Serve this sauce with steaks, barbecued ribs, and cold cuts. Since men like it so much, beer is suggested as a go-with.

Hot Sauce, Number II

Cooking time: 20 minutes

Yield: 2 cups

- 2 cups malt vinegar
- 1 teaspoon salt
- ½ teaspoon cayenne pepper or black pepper
- 1 tablespoon dry mustard
- 3 tablespoons sugar
- 2 tablespoons flour
- 2 tablespoons molasses
- 1 tablespoon crushed mixed pickling spices

METHOD:

1. Combine ingredients thoroughly. Bring to a quick boil.
2. Cook mixture 20 minutes. Cool to room temperature, and strain. Refrigerate.

NOTE:

A special sauce—of particular appeal to men. Always put on the table when serving *chili con carne* and other Mexican dishes.

Mustard Sauce

Cooking time: about 1 hour

Yield: 4 8-ounce jars

　1　cup sugar
3-4　tablespoons dry mustard
　2　tablespoons flour
　1　cup white vinegar
　2　egg yolks, beaten
　2　cups light cream
　　　salt
　⅛　teaspoon garlic powder (optional)

METHOD:

1. Mix sugar, mustard, and flour. Stir in vinegar to make a paste. Turn into top of double boiler.
2. Blend the yolks into the cream, add to paste in double boiler.
3. Cook over simmering water, stirring often.
4. Cook sauce for about 1 hour, until thick. Strain.
5. Add salt to taste, and garlic powder if desired. Seal in hot sterilized jars. Keep in refrigerator after jar is opened.

NOTE:

A savory sauce with fried fish. Good, too, with hot dogs and hamburgers.

Easy Mustard Sauce

Cooking time: 15 minutes

Yield: 1½ cups

　1　egg
　¼　cup sugar
　1　tablespoon dry mustard
　　　(or more to taste)
　1　tablespoon flour
　½　teaspoon salt
　1　cup undiluted canned beef broth
　½　cup cider vinegar
　　　pepper and salt

METHOD:

1. Beat egg and sugar together, beat in mustard, flour, and salt.

2. Stir in broth. Cook, and stir over moderate heat until mixture thickens.
3. Stir in vinegar, pepper, and salt to taste. Continue cooking until it reaches the thickness preferred. Pour in jar or container, and keep refrigerated.

NOTE:

Add a little of this sauce to your macaroni and cheese casserole for an extra zip.

Plum Sauce

Cooking time: 1 hour

Yield: 12 16-ounce jars

　1　teaspoon crushed red pepper flakes
　1　tablespoon mixed pickling spice
　1　tablespoon whole allspice
　1　teaspoon ground ginger
54　prune plums, about 6 pounds
　6　cups sugar
　6　cups vinegar

METHOD:

1. Combine spices and tie in a piece of cheesecloth.
2. Put all ingredients in large kettle, and cook over moderate heat for 1 hour, or until plums are soft and pits separate. Remove pits and cheesecloth with a slotted spoon.
3. Put sauce through a sieve or food mill. Seal in hot sterilized jars.

NOTE:

Hot or cold, Plum Sauce is marvelous with pork, ham, or veal.

Tomato Sauce, Number I

Cooking time: 3–4 hours

Yield: 12 16-ounce jars

36–40　ripe tomatoes, about 12 pounds
　5–6　tart medium apples, peeled, cored

and chopped, 1½ pounds
3 medium onions, 1 pound
12 garlic cloves, peeled and minced
4 cups cider vinegar
¼ cup salt
4 tablespoons whole allspice
1 tablespoon ground mace
1 tablespoon whole cloves
1 tablespoon crushed red pepper flakes
        or
¼ teaspoon cayenne pepper

METHOD:

1. Blanch tomatoes, rub or pull off skins, cut in quarters.
2. Use a large heavy kettle, and in it combine quartered tomatoes, chopped apples, sliced onions, garlic, vinegar, and salt.
3. Add spices tied in a piece of cheesecloth.
4. Boil mixture for 3 hours or more, until it is thick, dark, and aromatic.
5. Remove spice bag. Seal in hot sterilized jars.

NOTE:

Use this flavorful sauce in place of ordinary catsup or chili sauce. It is an excellent seller for fund-raising projects.

Tomato Sauce, Number II

Cooking time: 45 minutes

Yield: 2 16-ounce jars

3-4 very ripe tomatoes, about 1 pound
2 tart apples, about ½ pound
4 cups cider vinegar
3-4 garlic cloves, peeled
1 teaspoon salt
1 tablespoon sugar
1 shallot or onion, minced
2 chili peppers, seeded and chopped
3 lemons, juice of

METHOD:

1. Rinse tomatoes and apples, place together in a baking dish. Roast in a slow oven, 200 degrees, until very soft. Put through a sieve or food mill.
2. Add remaining ingredients, except lemon juice, in large kettle and cook 30 minutes. Strain through a sieve and return to kettle.
3. Stir in lemon juice, and cook mixture until it is as thick as heavy cream.
4. Cool. Seal in hot sterilized jars.

NOTE:

A good accompaniment to shrimp, hot or cold. Try it as a flavor enhancer in simple casseroles and Italian dishes. Spoon over omelets.

English Worcestershire Sauce

Cooking time: 2 hours

Yield: 8 16-ounce jars

6-7 tart cooking apples, cored and chopped, about 2 pounds
1 orange, seeded and cut up
4⅔ cups brown sugar, packed
4 tablespoons salt
2 tablespoons ground ginger
2 tablespoons ground cloves
1 teaspoon cayenne pepper
2 cups water
2 cups vinegar

METHOD:

1. Put all ingredients in a large heavy kettle, bring to a boil.
2. Reduce heat and simmer very gently for 2 hours, stirring often.
3. Cool. Put through a fine strainer (sauce should be very smooth), or process in a blender. Seal in hot sterilized bottles or jars.

NOTE:

This Worcestershire sauce tastes different from American varieties. It is good with hot and cold meats, and more than good with cheese dishes such as Welsh rabbit.

Salad Dressings

Boiled Salad Dressing

Cooking time: 10 minutes

Yield: 2 cups

1 can (14 ounces) condensed milk
2 tablespoons melted butter
1 teaspoon mustard
½ teaspoon pepper
1 egg white, beaten
2 cups white vinegar

METHOD:
1. Combine all ingredients, and mix well.
2. Bring to a boil, stirring continuously. Cook 10 minutes.
3. Cool, and refrigerate.

NOTE:
Can be used in the same way as mayonnaise. If desired, thin down with milk, cream, or fruit juice.

Old-Fashioned Boiled Dressing

Cooking time: 10 minutes

Yield: 2 cups

- 2 egg yolks, slightly beaten
- ¾ cup milk
- 2 tablespoons sugar
- 2 tablespoons flour
  dash of cayenne pepper
- 1 teaspoon salt
- 1 teaspoon dry mustard
- ¼ cup white vinegar
- 2 tablespoons soft butter

METHOD:

1. Mix egg yolks, milk, and dry ingredients in top of double boiler.
2. Place over simmering water, and stir in the vinegar.
3. Cook gently, stirring continuously, for 10 minutes.
4. As soon as mixture thickens, stir in the butter.
5. When mixture is thick and thoroughly blended, cool slightly. Store in refrigerator.

NOTE:

This is particularly delicious in fruit salads, chicken salads, and tunafish salads.

Easy Cooked Salad Dressing

Cooking time: 8–10 minutes

Yield: 1 8-ounce jar

- 2 tablespoons butter
- 6 tablespoons sugar
- 2 teaspoons salt
- 2 teaspoons prepared mustard
- 4 eggs
  pinch white pepper
- 1 cup white vinegar

METHOD:

1. Cream butter and sugar in a heavy saucepan until smooth. Cream in salt and mustard.
2. Beat in eggs.
3. Slowly stir in vinegar.
4. Cook over direct heat, stirring all the time.
5. As soon as mixture boils and thickens, remove from heat. Store in refrigerator.

NOTE:

Use as is, as dressing on potato salad or slaw. For use with other salads, thin with a little cream.

English Salad Cream

Cooking time: 15–20 minutes

Yield: about 2 cups

- 1 tablespoon dry mustard
- 1 tablespoon sugar
- 1 teaspoon flour
- ½ teaspoon salt
- 2 eggs, beaten
- ¾ cup white vinegar
- cream or milk

METHOD:

1. In the top of double boiler, thoroughly mix dry ingredients. Blend in eggs and vinegar.
2. Cook and stir over simmering water until thickened and smooth, 15–20 minutes.
3. Remove from heat, and cool for about 1 hour.
4. Add enough cream or milk to make approximately 2 cups of dressing.
5. Let cool. Store in refrigerator.

NOTE:

A simple but savory salad dressing, popular in England. It is good with fruit and molded salads.

French Dressing

Cooking time: none

Yield: ¾ cup

- ½ cup salad oil
- 2 tablespoons lemon juice
- 2 tablespoons white vinegar
- ½ teaspoon dry mustard
- ½ teaspoon paprika
- 1 teaspoon sugar
- few grains cayenne pepper

METHOD:

1. Put all ingredients in a screw-top jar, or in the blender.
2. Blend well. Always shake briskly before using.

NOTE:

French Dressing is the classic combination for salads and marinades. It can be varied many ways. Try adding the following ingredients:

CATSUP DRESSING—add ¼ cup catsup, 1 teaspoon Worcestershire sauce, 1 teaspoon grated onion.

ROQUEFORT DRESSING—add 4 tablespoons crumbled Roquefort cheese.

CHIFFONADE DRESSING—add 2 tablespoons chopped parsley, 2 tablespoons finely chopped onion, 1 chopped hard-boiled egg, ¼ cup chopped, cooked beets.

CHEF'S SALAD DRESSING—add 4–5 tablespoons crumbled Roquefort cheese, 1 teaspoon anchovy paste, juice of ½ lemon, ½ cup olive oil, 2 tablespoons vinegar, ½ clove of minced garlic, salt and pepper to taste.

SUMMER DRESSING—add 3 tablespoons orange juice, 3 tablespoons pineapple juice, and 3–4 teaspoons sugar.

Tomato Salad Dressing, Number I

Cooking time: none

Yield: 4½ cups

   2 cups good light olive oil
2½ tablespoons brown sugar
   1 teaspoon dry mustard
  ½ teaspoon salt
     pinch dried basil (optional)
  ½ cup vinegar
  ½ cup canned tomato sauce
   2 cloves garlic, halved

METHOD:
1. Use a wire whip to mix oil, sugar, and seasonings.
2. Beat in vinegar and tomato sauce. Stir in garlic.
3. Let stand overnight. Strain.
4. Pour into containers or jars, and store in refrigerator.

NOTE:
Good with all green salads. Nice with baked potato. Add to cheese and spaghetti dishes.

Tomato Salad Dressing, Number II

Cooking time: none

Yield: 4 cups

  ½ cup salad oil
  ½ cup white vinegar
  ½ cup sugar
   2 tablespoons grated onion
      or
   1 clove of garlic, minced
   1 can (10 ounces) condensed tomato soup
1½ teaspoons salt
 ¾ teaspoon dry mustard
  ½ teaspoon paprika
1½ tablespoons Worcestershire sauce

METHOD:
1. Combine all ingredients in screw-top jar or blender. Shake well to blend thoroughly.
2. Pour into container, and refrigerate.

NOTE:
An excellent dressing with shrimp cocktail or avocado salad.

129

Mayonnaise

Cooking time: none

Yield: 3 cups

  1 teaspoon salt
¼ teaspoon paprika
½ teaspoon dry mustard
   few grains cayenne pepper
  2 egg yolks
  2 tablespoons white vinegar
  2 cups salad oil
  2 tablespoons lemon juice
  1 tablespoon hot water

METHOD:
1. Use a rotary hand beater or an electric mixer to mix dry ingredients. Add egg yolks, and blend well.
2. Beat in vinegar.
3. Begin adding oil 1 teaspoon at a time, beating well after each addition.
4. After 3 teaspoons have been added, begin adding oil by tablespoons until 8–10 tablespoons have been added.
5. You can now increase your oil to 2–3 tablespoons at a time, still beating well with each addition.
6. When there are only 3–4 tablespoons oil left to blend in, add the lemon juice to the oil, and blend in together.
7. Beat in hot water last to make mayonnaise fluffy and decrease the oily appearance. Store in refrigerator.

NOTE:
The recipe for mayonnaise can be varied as follows:

FRUIT DRESSING—add ½ cup heavy cream, whipped, with 1 tablespoon sugar.

CUCUMBER DRESSING—add 1 cup diced and drained cucumber.

RUSSIAN DRESSING—add 1 chopped, hard-cooked egg, ¼ cup chili sauce, and 2 tablespoons chopped green pepper.

THOUSAND ISLAND DRESSING—add ½ cup bottled chili sauce, 3 hard-cooked eggs, finely chopped, 1 tablespoon minced onion, 1 tablespoon chopped dill pickles, 1 small green pepper, chopped, and ¼ cup chopped celery.

Papaya Seed Dressing

Cooking time: none

Yield: 3 cups

    1 cup tarragon vinegar or
       good white wine
    1 small white onion, cut up
    1 teaspoon seasoned salt (commercial
       blend of salt and spices)
    1 teaspoon dry mustard
    ½ cup sugar
    2 cups salad oil
    3 tablespoons fresh papaya seeds

METHOD:
1. Put vinegar, onion, seasonings, and sugar in blender container. Blend until smooth.
2. Add oil and papaya seeds. Process until seeds look like specks of coarse ground pepper. Store in refrigerator.

NOTE:
Papaya is a tropical fruit with a delicious, sweet-tart, musky taste. In this country papayas are available chiefly where grown—in Florida and Texas—and where there is a Spanish-speaking population.

This is an unusual dressing to be served on all sorts of salads; particularly good on fruit salads or with sliced tomatoes. If papaya is not in season, try making this dressing with poppy seeds—not the same flavor but very good.

Spiced Vinegar

Cooking time: 15 minutes

Yield: 4 16-ounce bottles

    8 cups cider vinegar
    2 tablespoons whole pickling spice
    4 tablespoons peppercorns
    4 tablespoons cracked ginger
           or
    1 teaspoon ground ginger
    ⅛ teaspoon cayenne pepper

METHOD:
1. Combine all the ingredients, and boil hard for 15 minutes.
2. Strain through several thicknesses of wet cheesecloth.
3. Seal in hot, sterilized bottles.

NOTE:
This tangy vinegar can be used in place of ordinary vinegar to pep up a great variety of recipes. Use it to thin down salad dressings. Or add just a drop or two to dips and spreads for extra flavor.

Bottles and corks can be bought in most stores that sell glassware.

131

Spiced and Candied Fruits

Christmas Apples

Cooking time: 45 minutes
Water bath: 10 minutes

Yield: 6 16-ounce jars

2 lemons
4 cups sugar
2 cups water
16 crab apples, stemmed, about 2 pounds
    red food coloring

Method:

1. Halve, seed, and thinly slice lemons. Combine with sugar and water in a heavy kettle.
2. Heat to boiling. Cook, skimming occasionally, until mixture becomes syrupy, about 5 minutes. Cool to lukewarm.
3. Place apples in syrup. Heat to boiling. Simmer slowly for 10 minutes. Allow apples to stand overnight in syrup.
4. The next day, heat mixture to boiling. Simmer slowly until apples look clear, about 30 minutes. Add a few drops of red food coloring for a deeper color. Seal in hot sterilized jars. Cook in a water bath, 10 minutes.

Note:

Serve in a ring around your Christmas turkey or use on your buffet table with a platter of cold meats.

Spiced Apricots

Cooking time: 20 minutes

Yield: 6 8-ounce jars

1 package (1 pound) dried apricots
cold water
3 cups white vinegar
2½ cups sugar
½ inch piece stick cinnamon
2 tablespoons whole cloves
2 tablespoons whole allspice

Method:

1. Cover apricots with cold water in a large bowl. Cover bowl with a towel. Allow to stand overnight. Drain water from apricots.
2. Combine 1½ cups vinegar, sugar, and spices, tied in a piece of cheesecloth, in heavy kettle.
3. Heat to boiling, slowly adding remaining 1½ cups vinegar. Add prepared apricots. Simmer 5 minutes.
4. Remove spice bag. Seal in hot sterilized jars.

Note:

Serve with ham, pork, cold cuts, and cottage cheese.

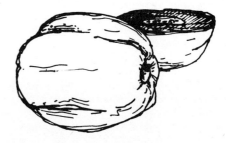

Spiced Cantaloupe

Cooking time: 1 hour

Yield: 6 16-ounce jars

3 ripe, firm cantaloupes, about 1 pound each
1½ teaspoons alum*
8 cups water
3 cups sugar
2 cups white vinegar
2 pieces stick cinnamon
1 tablespoon allspice
1½ teaspoons whole cloves

Method:

1. Pare and seed cantaloupe. Cut into 1-inch cubes, or use a melon-ball cutter.
2. Dissolve alum in water in a heavy kettle.
3. Heat to boiling. Add cantaloupe, and cook for 15 minutes. Drain cantaloupe, and wash well.
4. Combine sugar, vinegar, and spices tied in a piece of cheesecloth in the same kettle.
5. Heat to boiling. Add melon, and cook slowly until fruit is transparent, about 45 minutes.
6. Remove spice bag. Seal in hot sterilized jars.

Note:

Serve Spiced Cantaloupe with cold cuts. Or spear with toothpicks for an unusual cocktail-party hors d'oeuvre.

*Alum is an ingredient useful in home pickling to give crispness to melons and other foods. It can be bought in a drugstore.

Candied Ginger

Cooking time: 1 hour

Yield: 2 16-ounce jars

> 1 **pound fresh ginger root***
> **cold water**
> 2 **cups granulated sugar**
> 1 **cup water**
> 1 **cup superfine sugar**

METHOD:
1. Pare ginger root. Cut into thin slices, across the grain.
2. Cover with cold water in a saucepan.
3. Heat to boiling. Simmer 5 minutes. Drain ginger. Cover with cold water.
4. Heat to boiling. Simmer 5 minutes. Drain. Dry on paper towels.
5. Combine granulated sugar and 1 cup water in heavy kettle.
6. Heat to boiling. Boil 10 minutes or until a syrup forms.
7. Add ginger. Cook slowly, stirring often, until all syrup is absorbed, about 40 minutes. (Be sure ginger does not boil.)
8. Remove ginger from kettle, and place on wire racks to dry.
9. Roll ginger in superfine sugar sprinkled on waxed paper, and let ginger stand in sugar until it crystallizes.
10. Spoon into cold sterilized jars, and seal.

NOTE:

Candied Ginger is a lovely, unusual confection, nice to give as a gift packed in a decorative jar—it lasts for years in sealed airtight jars. The sugar left in the jars may be added to your cakes or sprinkled on top of coffee cakes on removal from the oven. Add a little to your curries while cooking.

*Ginger root is sold in stores that specialize in Oriental and Indian foods.

Imitation Preserved Ginger

Cooking time: 50 minutes

Yield: about 4 8-ounce jars

> 2 **pounds young carrots**
> **cold water**
> 2 **cups sugar**
> 6-10 **drops oil of ginger***
> **or**
> 1 **teaspoon cracked Jamaica ginger**
> 1 **lemon, juice of**

METHOD:
1. Peel carrots, and cut into one-inch pieces.
2. Place in a large saucepan. Cover with cold water.
3. Heat to boiling. Simmer until almost tender but not soft. Drain carrots.
4. Place sugar, 2 cups water, oil of ginger, and lemon juice in a heavy kettle.
5. Heat mixture to a boil. Cook until a syrup forms, about 10 minutes.
6. Add carrots, and simmer 10 minutes.
7. Take pan off heat and allow to cool. Then boil and cool carrots *twice more*.
8. Remove from heat and allow to cool. Pack into hot sterilized jars and seal.

NOTE:

When there is no ginger root on the market, try this recipe as an interesting substitute. A good recipe to have on hand if you like to cook Chinese dishes.

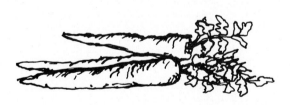

*Oil of ginger can be purchased at a drugstore.

Preserved Grapes

Cooking time: 45 minutes
Water bath: 20 minutes
Yield: 6 16-ounce jars

12 cups seedless grapes, stemmed,
   about 6 pounds
 3 cups water
12 cups sugar

METHOD:
1. Place grapes with water in a heavy kettle.
2. Heat, *very slowly,* until mixture is hot, but not boiling. Add sugar, slowly, stirring until sugar dissolves. (Stir with care so grapes will remain whole.) Cook, skimming several times, until syrup tests for set, about 30 minutes.
3. Pack grapes into hot sterilized jars with a slotted spoon. Cover to within ⅛-inch of top with hot syrup. Cook in a water bath 20 minutes. Keep refrigerated.

NOTE:
If you have an asbestos mat, this is a wonderful help in cooking this preserve, because it helps to distribute the heat evenly. A French recipe from Bar-le-Duc in Lorraine. This preserved fruit will stand on its own as a dessert if you have a *very* sweet tooth. Serve with sour cream.

Candied Kumquats

Cooking time: 1 hour
Yield: 8 8-ounce jars

2 cups sugar
2 cups water
⅛ teaspoon cream of tartar
6 jars (8 ounces each) Preserved
   Kumquats (page 136)
   granulated sugar

METHOD:
1. Combine 2 cups sugar, water, and cream of tartar in a heavy kettle. Heat to boiling. Add Preserved Kumquats.
2. Boil for 30 minutes. (This helps to plump the fruit.) Remove from heat. Prick the stem end of each kumquat with a sterilized needle. Allow the fruit to stand in syrup overnight.
3. The next day, heat to boiling. Cook 30 minutes. Drain kumquats in a sieve with a bowl underneath to catch the drippings.
4. Allow kumquats to dry, then roll in granulated sugar.
5. Pack in cold sterilized jars with wax paper lining between layers. Seal. Place leftover syrup in hot sterilized jars.

NOTE:
Kumquats are small, miniature oranges, plum shaped rather than round. They may be preserved in syrup, or preserved and then candied.

Candied Kumquats are delicious with ice cream or pound cake. Or slice and use to decorate gelatin salads and cake frostings. Leftover syrup can be used in fruit salads and as a glaze for a baked ham.

Preserved Kumquats

Cooking time: 1 hour 15 minutes

Yield: 6 8-ounce jars

**8 cups kumquats, about 2 pounds
cold water
3 cups granulated sugar
4 cups water**

METHOD:
1. Stem kumquats. Wash well in a colander. Place in heavy kettle with cold water to cover.
2. Heat to boiling. Cook for 15 minutes. Drain. Then repeat placing in cold water and boiling *twice more*.
3. Combine sugar and 4 cups water with kumquats in kettle.
4. Heat to boiling, stirring until sugar dissolves. Boil gently until fruit is transparent, about 30 minutes. (If using a candy thermometer, cook to 238 degrees.)
5. Remove kettle from heat. Cover, and allow to stand 30 minutes.
6. Pack into hot sterilized jars, being sure to cover kumquats with syrup, and seal jars.

NOTE:
Serve these kumquats with ham, chicken, or turkey.

Gingered Pears

Cooking time: 50 minutes

Yield: 10 16-ounce jars

**15 hard, unripe pears, peeled and cored, about 5 pounds
3 cups water
10 cups sugar
3 teaspoons lemon rind
6 tablespoons lemon juice
½ cup preserved ginger, thinly sliced
or
½ cup crystallized ginger, thinly sliced**

METHOD:
1. Cut pears into thin slices. Combine with water in heavy kettle.
2. Heat to boiling. Simmer until tender, about 20 minutes. Pour into large bowl.
3. Combine sugar and lemon rind and juice in same kettle. Stir until sugar dissolves. Add pears and ginger.
4. Cook, stirring often, until mixture thickens, and pears are transparent, about 30 minutes.
5. Spoon into hot sterilized jars, and seal.

NOTE:
Nice to serve with chicken and cheese, or with ham, pork, and meat sandwiches.

The most thoughtful gift in the world is the one that comes from your kitchen. These pretty Christmas packages contain Mincemeat (far left), Candied Ginger (top), Christmas Apples (middle), and Salted Pecans (lower right).

Candied Pineapple

Cooking time: 45 minutes

Yield: 8–10 slices

1 large ripe pineapple
  water
2 cups sugar
⅓ cup light corn syrup

METHOD:

1. Slice, peel, and core pineapple. Place in a large skillet and cover with water.
2. Heat to boiling. Simmer 15 minutes, or until pineapple is tender. Drain pineapple slices on paper towels; pour water out of skillet.
3. Stir sugar and corn syrup together in same skillet. Add pineapple slices. Simmer gently until fruit is transparent, about 30 minutes.
4. Allow pineapple slices to stand in syrup overnight. Drain on a wire rack. Allow to dry 2 hours.
5. Layer between rounds of waxed paper in cold sterilized jars, and seal.

NOTE:

If you wish to have green pineapple for decorating purposes, add a few drops of green food coloring to the syrup while cooking. This pineapple may be used for small Christmas cakes, decorating cookies, or just plain nibbling.

Spiced Prunes

Cooking time: 1 hour 15 minutes

Yield: 4 8-ounce jars

1 box (1 pound) prunes
3 cups cold tea
2 cups sugar
1 cup vinegar
1 teaspoon whole cloves
10 whole allspices
1 teaspoon ground mace

METHOD:

1. Place prunes in a large bowl, and cover with cold tea. Cover bowl. Allow to stand overnight.
2. The next day, cook prunes and tea in a large saucepan until prunes are tender, about 1 hour. Pack into hot sterilized jars with a slotted spoon.
3. Heat sugar, vinegar, and spices, tied in a piece of cheesecloth, to boiling in the same saucepan. Simmer 5 minutes.
4. Remove spice bag. Pour hot liquid over prunes. Seal immediately.

NOTE:

Use with all cold meats or cream cheese. Serve as hors d'oeuvres with cocktails, plain, or rolled in bacon strips and broiled.

Candied Orange, Lemon, or Grapefruit Peel

Cooking time: 1 hour 15 minutes

Yield: 8 8-ounce jars

    8 large oranges
            or
    12 large lemons
            or
    4 large grapefruit, about 2 pounds
       water to cover
    1½ cups water
       pinch of baking soda
    ¾ cup sugar
       additional sugar for coating

METHOD:

1. Peel rind from oranges, lemons, or grapefruits. Cut into lengthwise sections. Place peel in a heavy kettle. Cover with water, and add baking soda. (Baking soda softens the skins.)
2. Heat to boiling. Cook slowly until skins are soft, about 30 minutes. Drain peel, and scrape out the white pith with a teaspoon.
3. Heat ¾ cup sugar and 1½ cups water to boiling in same kettle. Boil 5 minutes to form a syrup. You may tint the syrup at this stage with yellow food coloring for lemons and grapefruit or add a drop of red for oranges. Add peel, and cook until syrup is almost absorbed, about 40 minutes, being careful that peel does not burn.
4. Drain peel onto sugar-lined wax paper. Roll peel to coat well. Allow to dry on wax paper.
5. Pack in cold sterilized jars, and seal immediately.

NOTE:

Use as a decoration on iced cakes and petits fours, or eat plain as candy. Packaged in dimestore brandy snifters, these candied peels make colorful gifts.

Spiced Orange Rings

Cooking time: 1 hour

Yield: 4 16-ounce jars

  6 large oranges, about 2 pounds
     water
1½ cups sugar
1½ cups white vinegar
  4 small pieces stick cinnamon
  2 teaspoons whole cloves

METHOD:

1. Cut oranges into ¼-inch slices, and seed. Place orange slices in a large heavy kettle, and cover with cold water.
2. Heat to boiling. Cook until fruit is tender, about 45 minutes. Drain in colander.
3. Heat sugar, vinegar, cinnamon, and whole cloves in same kettle. Heat to boiling. Add orange rings, a few at a time. Cook until rings are tender and clear, about 15 minutes.
4. Pack orange slices into hot sterilized jars. Boil syrup until thick and pour over oranges, dividing spices among jars. Seal immediately.

NOTE:

Serve with ham, pork, or roast duck.

Potted Raspberries

Cooking time: 10 minutes

Yield: 12 8-ounce glasses

16 cups fresh red raspberries,
     about 4 pounds
  2 tablespoons butter
  8 cups sugar, superfine

METHOD:

1. Wash and dry raspberries on paper towels. Rub the side and bottom of a heavy kettle with butter. Place raspberries in kettle.
2. Heat very slowly until berries start to bubble (do not boil). Add sugar, and stir until sugar dissolves.
3. Remove from heat, and beat with a wooden spoon for about 10 minutes. Seal in hot sterilized glasses.

NOTE:

Wonderful in small tarts eaten with whipped cream.

Nuts

Caramel Almonds

Cooking time: 10–15 minutes

Yield: 1 8-ounce jar

- ¼ cup granulated sugar
- ½ teaspoon salt
- pinch of ground cinnamon
- 1 cup whole almonds, blanched

METHOD:

1. Combine sugar, salt, and cinnamon in a heavy skillet. Add nuts.
2. Heat slowly, shaking pan often, until almonds brown lightly, and sugar turns golden.
3. Pour mixture onto a greased wooden

board, and separate nuts with two forks. Cool completely.

4. Pack into a fancy cold sterilized jar, and seal.

NOTE:

Do these nuts in small batches, because they should only be one layer deep in the frying pan. A Teflon-coated pan or heavy aluminum pan is the best type to use.

Fancy nuts make lovely Christmas gifts. I am often asked, "Do nuts keep well?" Yes, if sealed tightly and stored in a cold place, they will last for about two months.

Chocolate-Coated Almonds

Cooking time: 10 minutes

Yield: 3 8-ounce jars

4 milk-chocolate candy bars (about 1½ ounces each)
or
1 package (6 ounces) semisweet chocolate pieces
2 cups whole almonds, blanched

METHOD:

1. Break up candy bars in the top of a double boiler or in a heatproof bowl.
2. Place over simmering water, stirring well until chocolate melts.
3. Remove from heat. Cool slightly, and stir well.
4. Hold blanched almonds by the pointed end, and dip the rounded end into the chocolate. (I use a pair of sterilized tweezers in this operation.)
5. Place nuts on a wax paper-lined tray over a bowl of ice cubes, to cool nuts quickly.
6. Pack into cold sterilized jars, and seal.

NOTE:

Good as a light dessert accompaniment to hot, strong coffee. A nice decoration for petits fours, cupcakes, and cakes. Place these nuts in a fancy dish when friends drop by for a visit.

Pralined Almonds

Cooking time: 15 minutes

Yield: 4 8-ounce jars

4 cups whole almonds, blanched
2 tablespoons confectioners' (powdered) sugar

METHOD:

1. Arrange almonds in a single layer in a shallow baking pan. Coat with a light covering of powdered sugar, sprinkled through a sieve.
2. Bake in a very slow oven (225 degrees). Turn almonds and sprinkle with sugar again. Roast until nuts are caramel coated, about 15 minutes.
3. Cool nuts in pan. Spoon into cold sterilized jars, and seal.

NOTE:

This is a delicious nibble for a tea party or after dinner with port or sherry.

Candied Coconut Chips

Cooking time: 30 mimutes

Yield: 4 8-ounce jars

1 fresh coconut
1½ cups granulated sugar
¾ cup water

METHOD:

1. Remove meat from coconut shell, following directions in Toasted Coconut (below).
2. Remove thin brown skin, if desired, with a potato peeler. Slice coconut into thin strips with peeler.
3. Combine sugar and water in a heavy kettle. Stir until sugar dissolves. Add coconut slices.
4. Heat to boiling. Boil 20–30 minutes, stirring frequently. Continue boiling until water evaporates.
5. Pour into a foil-lined pan, and separate the strips with two forks. Cool completely.
6. Spoon into cold sterilized jars, and seal.

NOTE:

The dry coconut strips are nice served at cocktail parties, chopped fine over ice cream and cake frostings, or served with curry dishes as a condiment.

Toasted Coconut

Cooking time: 1 hour 15 minutes

Yield: about 4 8-ounce jars

1 fresh coconut

METHOD:

1. Pierce the three little dots at one end of the coconut with an ice pick. (The dots look like a monkey's face.)
2. Drain out the coconut milk, and save to use in making curry or for baking chicken or fish.
3. Heat coconut in slow oven (300 degrees) for 1 hour.
4. Remove coconut from oven. Cool. Crack by hitting with a rolling pin.
5. Using a potato peeler, cut into thin slices. (You can also remove the thin brown skin with potato peeler if you wish.) Or grate coconut pieces on a vegetable grater.
6. Spread coconut in a thin layer in a shallow baking dish.
7. Toast in a slow oven (300 degrees) for 15 minutes, or until coconut is a golden brown.
8. Cool in pan. Spoon into cold sterilized jars, and seal.

NOTE:

Use when making pies, cakes, and candy. Serve as a condiment with any curry dish. Sprinkle over a fresh fruit salad or ice cream.

Salted Pecans

Cooking time: 20 minutes

Yield: 2 8-ounce jars

- ½ cup butter
- 1 tablespoon salad oil
- 2 cups pecan halves
  salt

METHOD:

1. Melt butter in a large skillet (Teflon-coated pans are excellent for this). Skim off any milk solids that float to the top of the skillet.
2. Add salad oil, and heat.
3. Add pecans, and cook, stirring often, until they are slightly browned.
4. Remove pecans from skillet, and place on a clean towel.
5. Sprinkle with salt. Gather towel, and shake to coat nuts evenly with salt. Cool nuts completely.
6. Spoon into cold sterilized jars, and seal.

NOTE:

This method can also be used to prepare salted almonds. Both make welcome Christmas gifts. Serve them as a cocktail-party snack or chop them over pizza pies, casserole dishes, or Spanish rice. Remember to cut down the salt in your cooking if you intend to garnish with Salted Pecans.

Glazed Macadamia Nuts

Cooking time: 15 minutes

Yield: 2 8-ounce jars

- 1 can (6 ounces) whole macadamia nuts
- ½ cup granulated sugar
- 2 tablespoons butter or margarine
- ½ teaspoon vanilla extract

METHOD:

1. Combine nuts, sugar, and butter in a large heavy saucepan.
2. Cook over medium heat, stirring constantly, 15 minutes, or until sugar caramelizes, and nuts are well coated.
3. Remove from heat. Stir in vanilla.
4. Turn onto a greased board, and separate nuts with forks. Cool completely.
5. Spoon into cold sterilized jars, and seal.

NOTE:

These rich-tasting nuts are lovely sprinkled over vanilla ice cream or in dessert crêpes.

Caramel Walnut Squares

Cooking time: about 20 minutes

Yield: 4 16-ounce tins

- 3 cups granulated sugar
- 1 cup light cream
- 4 tablespoons butter or margarine
- ⅛ teaspoon baking soda
- 4 cups broken walnuts
- ½ teaspoon vanilla extract

METHOD:
1. Place 1 cup of the sugar in a large heavy saucepan.
2. Cook over low heat, stirring constantly until sugar melts and turns a light golden.
3. Add remaining 2 cups sugar and cream to melted sugar.
4. Cook, stirring constantly, until mixture reaches 248 degrees on a candy thermometer (hard-ball stage).
5. Stir in butter and soda. Cool for 10 minutes.
6. Add walnuts and vanilla, and beat until mixture thickens and loses its shine.
7. Pour into a greased 9 by 12-inch pan. Cool completely.
8. Cut into 1-inch squares.
9. Pack into sterilized coffee cans or 1-pound cookie tins.

NOTE:

This recipe is so popular, you'll want to make up several batches and give as gifts at Christmas.

Sugar Walnuts, Number I

Cooking time: about 7 minutes

Yield: 4 8-ounce jars

- 1 cup granulated sugar
- ⅓ cup milk
- ½ teaspoon ground cinnamon
- ½ teaspoon vanilla extract
- 4 cups walnut halves

METHOD:
1. Combine sugar and milk in a heavy saucepan.
2. Heat to boiling, stirring often. Boil until mixture reaches 236 degrees on a candy thermometer (soft-ball stage).
3. Remove from heat. Add cinnamon and vanilla. Beat well with a wooden spoon.
4. Add walnuts, and stir to coat well.
5. Turn onto a greased wooden board, and separate nuts with two forks. Cool completely.
6. Spoon into cold sterilized jars, and seal.

NOTE:

Try sprinkling these nuts over waffles. They are delicious also when eaten like candy.

Sugar Walnuts, Number II

Cooking time: about 10 minutes

Yield: 6 8-ounce jars

1½ cups granulated sugar
½ cup water
¼ cup honey
6 cups walnut halves
peppermint extract (optional)

METHOD:

1. Combine sugar and water in large heavy saucepan. Stir until sugar dissolves. Stir in honey.

2. Heat to boiling, stirring often. Boil until mixture reaches 236 degrees on a candy thermometer (soft-ball stage).

3. Remove from heat. Add nuts and extract, and stir with a wooden spoon until mixture hardens.

4. Turn onto a greased board, and separate nuts with two forks. Cool completely.

5. Spoon into cold sterilized jars, and seal.

NOTE:

Press nuts into centers of homemade fudge and fondant or stuff in dried apricot halves to accompany pork or ham.

Cheeses, Butters, Mincemeats, and Curds

Apple Butter, Number I

Cooking time: 50 minutes

Yield: 6 8-ounce jars

9-10 tart green apples, peeled, cored
and sliced, about 3 pounds
1 cup apple juice or apple cider
1½ cups sugar
½ teaspoon ground allspice
1 teaspoon cinnamon
¼ teaspoon ground cloves
⅛ teaspoon salt

METHOD:

1. Combine apple slices and juice, or cider, in a heavy kettle. Cover. Cook over moderate heat until apples are mushy, about 15 minutes. Strain.
2. Return to kettle, add sugar, spices, and salt. Mix well.
3. Cook and stir over moderate heat about 30–40 minutes, until mixture is thick.
4. Seal in hot sterilized jars.

NOTE:

For a good old-fashioned country breakfast, serve eggs, sausages, and hot biscuits with plenty of Apple Butter. This butter goes well at dinnertime with pork roast and pork chops, too.

Apple Butter, Number II

Cooking time: 1 hour

Yield: 8–10 8-ounce jars

15　green apples, about 5 pounds
　　apple cider
2½　cups sugar
¼　cup butter

METHOD:

1. Remove stem and blossom end from apples, cut in thick slices.
2. Add apple cider until you can just see it on top of apple slices. Bring to a boil, and cook 20 minutes, or until apples are soft.
3. Put through a sieve. Stir in sugar, and bring to a boil.
4. Reduce heat, continue to cook and stir apple mixture until thick, about 20 minutes.
5. Add butter. Continue to cook until mixture leaves sides of pan, about 20 minutes.
6. Seal in hot sterilized jars.

NOTE:

This is delicious with waffles, pancakes, or French toast.

Dutch Apple Butter

Cooking time: 50 minutes

Yield: 4 8-ounce jars

6　cooking apples
　　or
16　crab apples, 2 pounds
　　water
4　cups sugar
　　or
3　cups sugar and 1 cup honey
1　teaspoon ground nutmeg or pumpkin-pie
　　spice or ground cinnamon

METHOD:

1. Core apples, and cut into pieces. In a heavy kettle, combine apples with just enough water to keep from burning. Cover.
2. Heat to boiling. Cook over low heat until apples are mushy, about 15 minutes. Strain through a jelly bag, or press through a fine sieve.
3. Combine apple puree with sugar (or sugar and honey) and spice in the same kettle. Heat to boiling.
4. Cook, stirring often, until mixture is thick, about 30 minutes. Seal in hot sterilized jars.

NOTE:

A good filling for tarts. Or eat Dutch Apple Butter with a spoon with sour cream or ice cream or cottage creamed cheese. Or spread it on warm strips of pie crust and cover with cream or whipped cream.

Apricot Curd

Cooking time: 30 minutes

Yield: 3 8-ounce jars

12 fresh apricots, about 1 pound
       or
 3 cups dried apricots (soaked overnight),
       about 1 pound
       water
 2 cups sugar
 ½ cup butter
 2 lemons, juice of
 4 eggs, beaten

METHOD:
1. Halve, pit, dice apricots. Place in a large heavy saucepan. Cover apricots with water.
2. Heat to boiling. Cook until tender. Process in a blender, or press through a sieve.
3. Combine apricot puree, sugar, lemon juice, and butter in the top of a double boiler.
4. Cook over simmering water, stirring often, until sugar dissolves. Add beaten eggs. Cook, stirring constantly until mixture thickens, about 20 minutes. Seal in hot sterilized jars.

NOTE:
Delicious spread on pound cake and topped with whipped cream. Makes an ideal filling for tarts and layer cakes.

Blackberry Cheese

Cooking time: 10 minutes

Yield 6 8-ounce containers

 8 cups fresh blackberries, 2 quarts
       or
 8 cups stemmed black currants,
       about 3 pounds
       sugar

METHOD:
1. Rinse the berries and put in kettle with some moisture still clinging to them. Mash.
2. Cook until tender, then put through a sieve or food mill to make a puree.
3. Measure the puree or pulp and add 1 cup sugar for each cup pulp. This makes a sweet preserve. For a less sweet mixture, add ¾ cup sugar for each 1 cup fruit pulp. Mix well.
4. Cook over moderate heat, stirring all the time until mixture is very thick and pulls away from sides of pan.
5. Cool, and spoon into small plastic containers. Store in refrigerator.

NOTE:
Spread on slices of pound cake and top with sour cream.

A luncheon or tea becomes extra warm and personal with the hostess's own Quince Jelly, Lemon Curd, Chestnut Jam, and Peach-Macadamia Nut Conserve spooned into small tart shells and served on your prettiest tray.

Guava Butter

Cooking time: 30 minutes

Yield: 6 8-ounce jars

4 cans or jars (12 ounces) guavas
3 cups sugar
1 lemon, juice of
2 tablespoons grated ginger root
          or
1 teaspoon ground ginger
¼ teaspoon ground cinnamon
¼ teaspoon ground allspice

METHOD:

1. Press canned guavas through a food mill or process in an electric blender until smooth, to make 4 cups.
2. Combine guava puree with sugar, lemon juice, ginger, cinnamon, and allspice in a heavy kettle.
3. Heat to boiling. Simmer gently, stirring often, until mixture thickens and leaves sides of pan, about 30 minutes. Seal in hot sterilized jars.

NOTE:

For a delightful change, try Guava Butter with your usual breakfast toast or English muffin. Also nice to eat with yogurt and cottage cheese.

Lemon Curd

Cooking time: 15 minutes

Yield: 4 8-ounce glasses

4 large lemons
2 cups sugar
1 cup butter or margarine
4 eggs

METHOD:

1. Grate lemons, and squeeze. Place rind and juice in the top of a double boiler. Add sugar and butter.
2. Place double boiler over simmering water. Cook, stirring constantly, until the sugar and butter melt. Remove the top of the double boiler from the heat.
3. Beat eggs and gradually beat in hot mixture until smooth. Return the top of the double boiler to the heat. Cook, stirring constantly, until mixture coats the back of a spoon.
4. Remove from heat. Cover and allow to cool. Seal in hot sterilized glasses. Keep refrigerated.

NOTE:

Lemon Curd is a nice gift for a sick person—nourishing and fresh tasting. Also, very nice in layer cakes or small tarts, and should definitely be tried with breakfast toast and muffins.

Mock Lemon Curd

Cooking time: 10 minutes

Yield: 3 8-ounce glasses

2 large lemons, juice and rind
1 cup sugar
¼ cup butter or margarine
2 teaspoons cornstarch
2 eggs

METHOD:
1. Place lemon juice and rind in a large heavy saucepan with sugar and butter.
2. Heat slowly to boiling. Simmer a few minutes.
3. Blend cornstarch with 2 tablespoons cold water to make a smooth paste. Stir into boiling mixture.
4. Cook, stirring constantly, until mixture boils, 3 minutes. The mixture, when cooked, should coat the back of a spoon. It will thicken when cold.
5. Beat eggs in a bowl. Gradually beat in hot mixture until smooth.
6. Seal in hot sterilized glasses. Keep refrigerated.

NOTE:

This "poor man's lemon curd," somewhat cheaper than true lemon curd, nevertheless makes a nice filling for meringue shells.

Mango Butter

Cooking time: 50 minutes

Yield: 4 8-ounce jars

3 firm mangoes, about 3 pounds
1½ cups water
3 cups sugar
2 lemons, juice and rind
½ teaspoon ground nutmeg
½ teaspoon ground cinnamon
¼ teaspoon ground cloves
¼ teaspoon ground allspice

METHOD:
1. Peel, pit, and slice mangoes. Combine with water in a heavy kettle.
2. Heat to boiling. Cook until soft and mushy, about 20 minutes. Press through a sieve or process in an electric blender to make a puree.
3. Return mango puree to kettle with sugar, lemon rind and juice, and spices. Heat to boiling. Simmer gently, stirring often, until mixture thickens and leaves side of pan, about 30 minutes. Seal in hot sterilized jars.

NOTE:

Mango Butter combines deliciously with ice cream, yogurt, pancakes, and waffles, and it makes an excellent filling for layer cake.

Mincemeat

Cooking time: 40 minutes

Yield: 12 16-ounce jars

12 green tomatoes, peeled, about 3 pounds
9 large apples, peeled and cored,
   about 3 pounds
6 large pears, peeled and cored,
   about 2 pounds
3 large oranges, peeled and seeded
3 lemons, halved and seeded
7½ cups seedless raisins, 2½ pounds
1 cup brown sugar, packed
3 cups dark corn syrup or light molasses
1 cup cider vinegar
⅓ cup orange juice
⅓ cup lemon juice
2 tablespoons ground cinnamon
1½ teaspoons ground nutmeg
1½ teaspoons ground cloves
1½ teaspoons ground ginger
1½ teaspoons ground allspice
1½ teaspoons salt

METHOD:
1. Grind tomatoes, apples, pears, oranges, and lemons in a food grinder, using a fine blade, or process in an electric blender.
2. Combine in a heavy kettle. Add raisins, sugar, corn syrup, vinegar, and juices.
3. Heat to boiling. Simmer, stirring often, until mixture thickens, about 30 minutes. Add spices, and simmer 5 minutes. Seal in hot sterilized jars.

NOTE:
Mincemeat makes the perfect Christmas pie. It is also just as tasty in a tart. For a summer dessert surprise, combine Mincemeat and French vanilla ice cream, pour into a pie tin lined with graham-cracker crust, and freeze.

English-Style Mincemeat

Cooking time: none

Yield: 8 16-ounce jars

1 pound beef suet, ground
3 large cooking apples, peeled, cored, and chopped, 1 pound
4 lemons, juice and rind
4½ cups dried currants, 1½ pounds
3 cups dark raisins, 1 pound
1½ cups mixed candied peels and cherries, ¾ pound
1½ cups almonds, blanched and slivered
4⅔ cups brown sugar
1 tablespoon ground nutmeg
1 tablespoon ground ginger
1 tablespoon salt
1 cup raisin wine or muscatel
½ cup brandy

METHOD:
1. Combine suet, apples, lemon rind and juice, currants, raisins, candied peels and cherries, and almonds in a very large bowl. Blend in sugar, spice, salt, wine, and brandy. Cover, and allow to stand overnight.
2. The next day, seal in hot sterilized jars. Store in a cool dark place or refrigerate.

NOTE:
When required for pies, empty jar into a prepared pie shell and add a little more brandy, if desired. Top with pastry and bake. This mincemeat keeps well!

Parsley Honey

Cooking time: 40 minutes

Yield: 3 8-ounce glasses

3 cups fresh parsley sprigs
3 cups water
2 cups sugar
2 teaspoons vinegar

METHOD:

1. Chop parsley, and combine with water in a heavy kettle.
2. Heat to boiling. Boil until water reduces to 2 cups, about 15 minutes. Strain liquid, and discard parsley.
3. Combine strained liquid and sugar in kettle. Stir until sugar dissolves. Add vinegar.
4. Heat to boiling. Cook until mixture is a clear, honeylike consistency, about 25 minutes. Seal in hot sterilized glasses.

NOTE:

Mix Parsley Honey with an equal part of mayonnaise for fruit salads.

Pineapple Honey

Cooking time: 2 hours

Yield: 8–9 8-ounce jars

2 large, very ripe pineapples, peeled
1 lemon, quartered
6 cups sugar
dash of salt

METHOD:

1. Core the pineapple, and be sure all the eyes are scooped out. Cut into small pieces.
2. Put cut-up pineapple and lemon in blender, and process until finely chopped. Or run through a food grinder, using a fine blade.
3. Add sugar, mix well, and let stand overnight in a heavy kettle.
4. The next day, add dash of salt. Cook over very low heat for about two hours, or until very thick. Stir frequently to prevent scorching.
5. Seal in hot sterilized jars.

NOTE:

For a special dessert, mix Pineapple Honey with an equal amount of sour cream and serve cold. Spoon over little rolled crêpes, and serve warm. Also delicious with hot biscuits and butter.

Quince Cheese

Cooking time: 1 hour 20 minutes

Yield: 4 8-ounce jars

6 quinces, peeled, halved, cored, and sliced, about 1 pound

¼ cup water

3 large cooking apples, peeled, cored, and chopped, about 1 pound

4 cups sugar

METHOD:

1. Combine quinces with water in a heavy saucepan. Cook until very soft, about 1 hour.
2. Press through a sieve, or process in an electric blender.
3. Combine quince puree with chopped apples and sugar in a heavy kettle.
4. Heat, stirring until sugar dissolves, to boiling. Boil rapidly until set is reached, about 20 minutes. Seal in hot sterilized jars, and refrigerate.

NOTE:

Eat with cream, ice cream, cake, cheese, sour cream, or yogurt.

Index